TALES OF MADISON

Historical Sketches on
Jackson & Madison County, Tennessee

HARBERT ALEXANDER
Illustrations by Richard Brown

Hillsboro Press
PROVIDENCE PUBLISHING CORPORATION
FRANKLIN, TENNESSEE

TENNESSEE HERITAGE LIBRARY

Printed in the United States of America

06   05   04   03   02   1   2   3   4   5

Library of Congress Catalog Card Number: 2002105624

ISBN: 1-57736-265-9

Cover design by Gary Bozeman

Cover and text illustrations by Richard Brown

Hillsboro Press
PROVIDENCE PUBLISHING CORPORATION

238 Seaboard Lane • Franklin, Tennessee 37067
800-321-5692
www.providencepubcorp.com

CONTENTS

PREFACE & ACKNOWLEDGMENTS

For more than three decades I have been telling the story of the early history of Jackson and Madison County. As I told the old stories to civic clubs and school groups, I began to feel like I was a part of the history. Could I have been on old engine No. 638 with Casey Jones and Sim Webb on their way to destiny at Vaughn, Mississippi? It almost seemed that way. Did I vote against Davy Crockett in 1835 and send him west to the Alamo? I felt like I had! Or was I one of those young boys in the Sixth Tennessee Infantry who was killed in front of the Hornet's Nest at Shiloh? I could almost feel the warm sunshine of that April morning so long ago.

Some years ago a friend came back from Virginia, eager to tell me about her trip. "They have so much history there. I wish we did, too!" Certainly Virginia does have a lot of history. But so does West Tennessee. You just have to be aware of it. As a boy I picked up arrowheads where the First Baptist Church is now located. Civil War bullets and buckles could be found along North Highland Avenue. Fading paint on downtown buildings reveals signs for carriages and horse collars. Our history is all around us—just open your eyes.

Our history is unique in that there is a great deal of it compressed into a short period of time. Our first settlers came here less than two hundred years ago. Thus it would be possible for a person living today to have known one of the first settlers! Contrast this with the fact that native Americans lived here more than eight thousand years ago, and you realize how much history we have for such a short time span.

And our history is colorful because of the type of people who settled here. Our first settlers were part of the westward migration, the wave of people who began at Plymouth Rock and ended up all the way across the continent in California. Historians call this Manifest Destiny, and West Tennessee was right in the middle of it. For this reason, I sometimes refer to early days in West Tennessee as the "New West," rather than the "Old South."

Emma Inman Williams was my history teacher in high school. It would be years later that I began to appreciate her. In 1946 she wrote *Historic Madison*. In 1988 she co-authored *Jackson & Madison County: A Pictorial History*. To promote the book, I began taking her to local civic clubs. I would make a speech on our early history, and she would answer questions about the book. One day we gave a program at The Hut restaurant. When I was through with my speech and everyone was gone, she looked up at me and said, "You know, you've got that part about Davy Crockett's election all wrong. You've got Dr. Butler and Adam Huntsman backwards. You've got them mixed up!" I was sick. She was still my history teacher, even after all those years, and to get it wrong in front of her was unthinkable. Then she gave me a hug and a big grin and said, "But, oh you tell it so good." That was when I realized that I had become Jackson's storyteller.

There is a tradition that Indian tribes kept their history alive by selecting one of the elders to tell the history of their people to the children of the tribe. In a like manner, this is what I do today. I am our storyteller!

Emma Inman Williams was our best historian. When she wrote *Historic Madison*, she ensured that our early history would be preserved. She was our first county historian. When she died I became the county historian. We were different—she was a writer, and I was a storyteller. But in our own way we were keeping our history alive. As new generations came along, *Historic Madison* was long out of print. *Tales of Madison* is my way of keeping the story alive.

Madison County has many historians who in their own way help to keep the past alive. We are lucky to have them. Jack Woods and Robert Taylor in the Tennessee Room at the Jackson Madison County Library help people every day to trace their ancestors or answer a question about Madison County. They are a great resource. Jonathan K. T. Smith has kept the history of Riverside Cemetery alive. In his own quiet way he has written more than eighty manuscripts on Madison County history. The John Ingram Bivouac of the Sons of Confederate Veterans have restored and preserved Britton Lane and Salem Cemetery, our two Civil War battlefields. Jerry Lessenberry has been the spirit of Britton Lane, while Malcolm Wilcox has done the same for Salem Cemetery. What if we forgot to remember!

There are many more who never forgot. Clark Shaw helps to keep the memories of Casey Jones alive. Mark Norton, Mary Kwas, and Bob Mainfort did a lot more for the Pinson Mounds than their paychecks required. Dr. George Edwards found the Boone inscriptions and kept that story alive. Molly Stansell owns the land where James Coble is buried and let me walk over the land where he was killed. D. N. English is our best historian of downtown buildings and the stories that surround them. John Long preserves old fire engines and their history, while Eddie Ashmore is our best historian of Jackson's police force and days of law and order. Old friend Jim Driver catches me on the street and tells me more about train wrecks and historical characters than I can remember. How lucky we are to have all of them, and so many more.

Best of all is my associate Regina Barnhill who has typed all of my stories through the years. And even more, she believed in me and liked what I wrote. This book would not be possible without her.

INTRODUCTION
Jackson and Madison County History

Before the coming of the first settlers, Jackson and West Tennessee were occupied by pre-historic Indian tribes who camped and hunted here as early as 9,000 B.C. Madison County is famous for Pinson Mounds State Park located just south of Jackson. The park includes seventeen Indian mounds, one of which is the second largest in the United States. In addition, the Denmark Mounds west of Jackson are on the National Historic Register.

Tennessee came into the union in 1796; however, there would be no settlers in West Tennessee for another twenty years until the treaty with the Chickasaw Indians was signed in 1816. Jackson grew in size as a frontier town as pioneer settlers moved through. Our early pioneer ancestors were restless in nature and many of them continued on across the country as a part of what today's historians call "Manifest Destiny," or the settling of the country. In the 1840s, many West Tennesseeans moved on to Texas in search of cheaper land to raise cotton or as a part of the Texas Independence movement.

Today it is hard to imagine that Jackson was once a port city. For many years, however, transportation in Jackson

Davy Crockett.

centered around the Forked Deer River which was used to transport agricultural products to ports down stream on flat bottomed boats, keel boats, and small steamboats.

Frontier hero Davy Crockett represented Jackson for twelve years while serving in the state legislature and as a member of the U.S. House of Representatives in Washington. When he was defeated in 1835 he made an angry speech on the courthouse steps which ended with the words, "The rest of you can go to hell, for I am going to Texas." A year later he was dead at the Alamo. Another Jacksonian, Micajah Autry, also died as a soldier at the Alamo.

Jackson continued to grow during the decades leading up to the Civil War, with frontier life interrupted only by brief periods of war with the Seminole Indians and the war against Mexico. During the Civil War, a number of small battles or skirmishes occurred in the vicinity of Jackson. The Battle of Britton Lane, where raiding Confederate Cavalry units under General Frank C. Armstrong clashed with Federal infantry leaving more than 170 Confederate dead, is commemorated in the Denmark area with a small park. Another small skirmish occurred east of Jackson at Old Salem Cemetery as part of Nathan Bedford Forrest's West Tennessee Raid. There were two Confederate generals from Jackson—Alexander W. Campbell and William H. "Red" Jackson.

Jackson was occupied by Federal troops for exactly one year from April 1862 to April 1863. Federal raiders demanded ransom money in 1864 with a threat of burning Jackson; even though the ransom was paid, most of downtown Jackson was burned!

The town of Denmark, west of Jackson, once rivaled Jackson for prominence and size. A number of fires, tornadoes, and the relocation of the railroad spelled its demise. Today only a few houses remain along with a historic antebellum Presbyterian church.

The first railroad appeared in Jackson in 1858, coming from Columbus, Mississippi. Judge Milton Brown was the most prominent individual associated with the coming of the railroad to Jackson. The railroad brought much progress to West Tennessee in the years after the war, creating a labor base that would be used in later years for industrial development. I. B. Tigrett, a Jacksonian, was the president of Gulf, Mobile and Ohio Railroad, which boasted three thousand miles of track. In addition, the legendary Casey Jones lived here. His house and many of his effects are preserved in the Casey Jones Village.

Jackson has been the home of several musicians with national prominence. Included among them are Sonny Boy Williamson, a legendary blues and harmonica artist; Big Maybelle, a gospel and blues recording artist; and the legendary Carl Perkins—Mr. "Blue Suede Shoes."

Jackson, known since the 1930s as the Hub City, continues to grow and thrive today as a city with a regional population of more than one hundred thousand people. Even though it has a rich past, most Jacksonians feel the best is yet to come.

EARLY TOWNS
IN MADISON COUNTY

Madison County was formed on November 7, 1821, along with Carroll and Henderson Counties. The county was in the form of a perfect square with each side twenty-five miles in length, giving it an area of six hundred twenty-five square miles. The county was reduced in size in 1871 and again in 1879 when Crockett and Chester Counties were formed.

Jackson is the largest town in Madison County. Originally named Alexandria, the name was changed to Jackson on August 17, 1822. The first settlers came here in 1819, settling east of Jackson on Cotton Grove Road. The settlement was named Cotton Gin Grove. The next year four more families arrived and settled near the Forked Deer River where the West Tennessee Experiment Station is currently located. One of the settlers was a land grant surveyor named Adam Rankin Alexander. Thus this settlement, Alexandria, was named for him. Another Tennessee town was already named Alexandria, so the name was changed to honor Andrew Jackson whose sister-in-law Jane Hays lived here. Fifty-four acres were surveyed in August 1822 and divided into one hundred and four lots.

Today's downtown district was selected as a compromise site, situated roughly between Alexandria and Cotton Gin Grove. Twenty dollars was spent for whiskey to encourage bidding. Within one week, all of the lots were sold with the city realizing a profit of $19,202. Prices ranged from $31.00 to $503.00, with the most expensive sites being located closest to the center of the plot where the future courthouse would be located. Soon the courthouse was constructed at a cost of $135, along with a jail at a cost of $95. (Compare that to the eighteen million dollars we Jacksonians just spent for a new city hall and jail.) Jackson was up and running. In years to come it would become the home of a dynamic railroad industry, followed by the industries that are here today, such as Procter and Gamble, Porter Cable, and Owens Corning Fiberglass Corporation. While Jackson was growing, other Madison county towns and communities were established. Some of them prospered, many did not.

Though Henderson is now the county seat of Chester County, it was originally located in the southeastern part of Madison County. It was first named Dayton, then Henderson City, and Henderson Station before settling on Henderson. At first Henderson was little more than a stop on the Mobile and Ohio Railroad. Several stores located there in 1860, but the town experienced little growth until the 1870s when the town could boast of three hundred inhabitants, three churches, a drug store, saddle shop, livery, and blacksmith. In addition there were three saloons. Two newspapers were published there—the *Henderson Advocate* and the *Madison County Herald*. In 1871, the Henderson Masonic Male and Female Institute was chartered. By 1876, the college had 166 students.

By 1875 there was movement to create a new county out of a portion of Madison, Henderson, Hardeman, and McNairy Counties. The new county was to be named Wisdom County. In 1879, the name was changed to Chester County in honor of Colonel Robert I. Chester, one of Jackson's founding fathers.

Thus the early history of Henderson, from its birth to 1879, was a part of the history of Madison County. If Henderson were still a part of Madison County, it would be our second largest settlement.

Established in 1825, the community of Medon had several early names. Its first name, Frozen Oak, was somewhat colorful, commemorating a hunter who crawled into a hollow tree during a blizzard and froze to death. By 1834 the village was called Clover Creek. Finally the name was changed to Medon. Tradition tells the story of an early Irishman who lived there. When he returned home from a job, he would thump his chest and say "Me Done," hence today's name. Medon was incorporated in 1852. The first mayor was Dr. Joseph Stewart. Soon the stagecoach began running through the main street, stopping at the Stage Tavern operated by Peter Swink. Like Jackson, Medon plotted a center district and sold thirty-nine lots at auction. By 1880, the town had a population of 175 people. In 1875, the Medon Academy opened in the Masonic building. Stores and churches were built to accommodate its citizens. Today Medon has only a few stores. Nevertheless, 177 years after its founding, the community of Medon still remains.

First known as Harrisburg, Malesus was settled by the Horton, McKnight, Dunbar, Fulbright, Young, Day, Loftin, Hill, and Woodson families. Life in the community centered around two early churches—the Cane Creek Baptist Church organized in 1822 followed by the Ebenezer Methodist Church. Another Methodist church was built in 1869 named Black Jack's Meeting House. Although the community has grown and prospered and still retains much of its early origins, Malesus now seems to be very much a part of Jackson.

Mercer was begun in 1888 by T. B. Mercer at a site where the stage road crossed the newly laid track of the Tennessee Midland Railroad. Deciding that this was a good place for a town, Mercer erected a store near the cabin of Eaton Bond. In 1894 a railroad station was built. Because some name had to appear on the railroad timetable, the

Denmark Presbyterian Church.

railroad superintendent named the town Mercer. In 1893, the O. G. Gardner Lumber Company was opened and soon covered twelve acres. Of the Methodist, Baptist, and Presbyterian churches there, the oldest is the Methodist dating to 1894. The first school was located in the old Ebenezer Church. The church was not centrally located, so a new building was constructed. Many townspeople named it "Folly College." The Bank of Mercer was located in the downtown district but failed on May 18, 1933. Another colorful building, the Mercer Opera House, burned in recent years. Today Mercer has two stores, a restaurant, and a cotton gin. The population seems to grow in the fall when cotton comes to the gin or in November when deer season opens. It is not as large as it used to be, but many believe it has the best hamburgers in Madison County!

The history of Denmark is quite a story. For many years it seemed that it would equal Jackson in size. But history dealt it a cruel fate. Few people have traveled to Denmark or even know where it is. It is located about ten miles southwest of Jackson. Denmark sits on an old Indian trail that ran from Kentucky to Memphis. Once the site of a large Indian village, four mounds still mark the site. The first settlement was on a bluff over Big Black Creek at a site known as Reid's Old Mill. Two brothers named Harbert had a store there. In the 1830s, they moved their store to where the town is currently located. By 1840 there were eight stores there along with John Wray's grocery store, a toggery or whiskey store, and the Meriwether and Jett Hotel. The stagecoach stopped here on the way to Memphis. The 1850s were the crowning point in its history. By this time it was one of the most ambitious and promising towns in West Tennessee. Interest centered around religion and education. Prosperous Presbyterians built a large church, and the Methodists soon followed. As a mark of their prosperity, the Presbyterians paid their minister Rev. Cyrus Caldwell twelve hundred dollars a year, an unheard of salary for the time. Early church records tell of a much stricter life for church members. One such Presbyterian was called before the congregation and made to apologize for fighting, under threat of being removed from the church roles. The town had a Masonic Lodge with 154 members, a company of National Guards, and a brass band.

In 1831, just one year after the town was incorporated, the Denmark Male and Female Academy was chartered. At the end of the first year, thirty-five students participated in the closing exercises. In 1850 a new female academy was built. Both schools had about 150 students, many coming from adjoining counties and even from North Mississippi.

By 1872, the town seemed to grow smaller. At the center of the town were three hardware and grocery stores named for their owners—McKissack & Burton, Bryan, and Duncan. W. J. Hudson manufactured carriages, wagons, and buggies. Dr. John Tyson was a druggist and physician.

A. C. Burgess made coaches, buggies, and furniture. In addition, he served as the undertaker.

Dreams of the railroad coming to Denmark led to hopes for a new prosperity, yet soon spelled its doom. The Mobile and Ohio and the Mississippi Central and Tennessee Railroads came to Jackson and bypassed Denmark. In 1872 the citizens raised twenty-five thousand dollars for a line to be known as the Denmark, Brownsville and Durhamville Railroad. This venture failed with only one mile built in a field west of Brownsville. Following this the citizens refused to raise three thousand dollars for the Tennessee Midland Railroad, believing it would have to come through the town anyway. They were wrong, and the line was built one mile south through Mercer. The little town began to decline as Mercer prospered.

Fires also played a large part in its failure. In 1860, seventeen stores burned. In 1867 a fire destroyed most of the business district including the stores of Reid, McKissack & Burton, Neely, and Meriwether. In 1903 three stores burned. Twelve other buildings and a cotton gin have burned since 1924. Today only a few buildings remain. The Presbyterian Church still stands though it has no congregation. Across the street is a new post office and two homes. Mrs. Robert Hardee, the postmistress, lives in a house built by the Harbert brothers. Louise Stevens lives next door in the home of her uncle, Stevie Carter, who helped to preserve much of the town's history.

There are three cemeteries in Denmark—the Presbyterian, Methodist, and Old Soldiers cemeteries. In the spring jonquils grow in the old fields around the tombstones and whisper of better times and hopes of long ago.

Towns such as Gilmore and Hanley no longer exist. But, like Jackson, they were early villages with dreams of great things. Recently, a man from Mobile, Alabama, called me to inquire about Gilmore. He was a brick collector. Decades ago, bricks had the name of the town where they were made imprinted on the top. He sent me one of the Gilmore bricks. The name was unfamiliar to me. Robert Taylor in the Tennessee Room of the Jackson-Madison County Library researched the name and found that it was located just north of Jackson close to Dyer Creek on the Old Medina Road. Though no town exists there, the name is still on area maps.

I have a letter written by my great-grandmother dated 1894. The postmark is from Hanley, Tennessee. Knowing that she had lived near Woodland, on the edge of Haywood County, I began questioning some area residents. They remembered the old post office, where the letter was post-marked, just across the road from Woodland Church. However, no trace of the old post office remains.

Cotton Gin Grove was our first community; it was settled in 1819. By 1834 it had a post office and a stage-coach stop. Adam Huntsman, the lawyer who defeated Davy Crockett, is buried there in the Old Salem Cemetery. The cemetery is the only reminder of that community. Huntsman's home site is just east of the cemetery. In effect, Cotton Gin Grove began its move toward obscurity when Jackson was formed in 1822.

Poplar Oaks was a small community eight miles north of Jackson on the Christmasville Road near where the Pleasant Hill Church stood. It was settled just prior to 1828. This is yet another small community that few people know of or have visited.

Spring Creek was once a thriving village. It grew up around the Haughton grist and flourmill. It is located about thirteen miles east of Jackson. The road leading to Jackson was so rough and sandy that people chose to shop at home rather than risk the journey. It was incorporated in 1854. By 1872 five hundred people lived there with six stores, Masonic Lodge Number 193, and a Cumberland Presbyterian Church incorporated in 1865. Along with the stores there were two schools—a beautiful three-story building which housed the Madison College and the Springdale Institute founded by Major Jesse Taylor in 1870.

Huntersville is located west of Jackson on the road to Brownsville not far from the airport. It is named for Doctor John Hunter, described as a saddle-pocket physician. Educated in Edinburgh, Scotland, he practiced medicine for years before he died of yellow fever in 1876. The town was located at the intersection of Jackson and Brownsville Road and Denmark to Poplar Corner Ferry Road. Two churches played a large part in the life of the community. Andrews Chapel, named for Bishop Andrews, was organized in the early 1820s. Major James Meriwether was a member of the committee to have a house of worship built. He had the logs hewn by hand and the lumber cut with a rip saw from the trees of the nearby forest, using slave labor to do all the work. The original building has been preserved and is still used as a place of worship. The congregation included members of the Davis, Transou, Witherspoon, Meriwether, Henning, Crittenden, Blackard, Chandler, and Valentine families.

The Baptists of the community organized the Ararat Church "just after the stars fell" (referring to a large meteor shower), long before the Civil War and built a house near the old Joe Henning home north of Huntersville. After the Civil War the church was moved to the present site. Many slaves in the community were baptized by the frontier missionary Obediah Dodson and they were members of the Ararat Church until they organized and built their own Bethlehem Church. Among the other families not already mentioned who contributed to the life of the community include the Coles, Iveys, Ingrams, Tysons, Murtaughs, Hoppers, Perrys, Pegues, and Strains.

After Dr. Hunter's death, Matt Wyley took over his store and also served as the first postmaster. The Post Office Department named the town Andrews Chapel for the nearby Methodist church. The two names caused confusion through the years, but the original name persisted. Today, however, the name remains Huntersville.

Mason's Wells was a health resort in the southeastern corner of Madison County. It was described as being located ten miles southeast of Jackson within four miles of Bear Creek. It was opened in 1861 by Joseph Mason. Visitors enjoyed the medicinal value of the iron and salts in the spring water. Guests could expect to find good water, good rooms, and a ballroom. The resort was reopened after the Civil War when newspaper ads reported that invalids would find a blessing near at hand in the waters of Mason's Wells.

Second only in size and importance to Jackson is the town of Bemis. As the nineteenth century neared its close, the Bemis Brothers Bag Company announced plans to move south and build mills that could supply their bag factories with goods of uniform quality. The mill was to be located on a southern site close to the cotton fields for the raw materials and on a good railroad line that provided quick service to their bag factories at New Orleans, Omaha, St. Louis, Minneapolis, San Francisco, and Indianapolis. Above all, the site needed to be close to an abundant labor supply. Officials of the Illinois Central Railroad began work to get the site located near their lines. Finally West Tennessee was settled on as a site which satisfied the Bemis requirements. At this time, Jackson was not designated as the site. A group of citizens headed by Stokley Hays, one of Jackson's most prominent citizens, and Mark Mathews, minister of the First Presbyterian Church, asked the county court to purchase three hundred acres of land. The site was known as the H. E. Jackson Plantation, three miles south of Jackson. The land was priced at six thousand dollars. The land would be donated to Bemis if they would agree to build a twenty-thousand-spindle cotton mill with a village located around it.

The county court was not as far sighted as Hays and Matthews and almost voted it down. On January 2, 1900, the court met to consider the purchase. The vote was twenty for and fifteen against. The chairman, believing that a three-fifths vote was necessary, declared the motion failed. When he was informed that only a simple majority was needed, he reconvened the court for an afternoon session.

This time nineteen voted for and fifteen against and the motion carried. Bemis accepted the land and construction began on the site. By the summer of 1901 the mill was in full operation. In 1905 a second mill was added.

Judson Bemis, president of Bemis Brothers Bag Company, created the mill site. His son Albert Farwell Bemis was the mind behind the project to build a model mill town. He was a graduate of Massachusetts Institute of Technology (MIT) with a degree in civil engineering. He enlisted the help of two architects, Andrew Hepburn and Arthur Schurcliff, to design the town. Years later these two architects would become famous for the restoration of Colonial Williamsburg.

Bemis the town was developed in a manner similar to other textile mill towns in the Carolinas. The heart of the village was the mill, a four-story structure designed by Lockwood, Greene and Company. The town was constructed around the mill in two separate time periods. The first period began in 1900 and lasted until 1914 when World War I interrupted. In addition to homes for the mill workers, a company store, a church, schools, a YMCA building, and a public bathhouse were constructed. The second period lasted from 1918 to 1926, and saw the construction of two additional housing developments, a park, an auditorium, stores, and another school. The only significant structure built after this was a new YMCA in 1940.

The social life of Bemis was governed to a large extent by the company. A Union Church, built by the company, served all denominations until they built their own churches. The company store provided postal and banking services. Recreational activities were coordinated through the YMCA. A doctor's office and drug store came later.

J. B. Young was the first resident manager of the Bemis textile mill. He would be followed by his son Fred Young and his grandson Fred Young Jr. They were company managers for more than sixty years. Much of the town's prosperity can be attributed to their leadership.

In the 1960s, textile plants across the South began to close their doors. The concept of Bemis as a mill village ended when the employees were offered the chance to buy their homes from the company. Eventually the mill was sold to an individual from Pakistan before finally closing its doors.

Today the mill and the surrounding village remain as a reminder of a model textile village. Its houses are protected under historical zoning codes. On May 20, 2000, the town celebrated its one hundredth anniversary with a ribbon cutting at the Bemis Historical Society Museum.

PINSON AND
THE PINSON MOUNDS

Eleven miles south of Jackson, sitting on Highway 45 South, is the town of Pinson. The town began on the land of A. S. Rogers. Prior to the development of the town, the area was prosperous farmland. Nearby was a large store owned by Rogers and C. H. Hearn. Rogers and E. R. Lancaster built a steam mill saw operation and other buildings followed. Lancaster opened a post office and by 1834, Mount Pinson was listed as one of the post offices of the Western District. The first school was begun in 1867 by Rev. John McCoy. A Baptist church soon followed with Rev. Levin Savage as the first minister. Next came the Methodists with Rev. E. L. Fisher serving as the first pastor.

Rogers and Hearn continued to operate their store with merchandise brought in from Memphis, Louisville, Philadelphia, and New York. The merchandise was shipped to Jackson or Perryville on the Tennessee River and hauled by wagons to Pinson. In 1859 they bought more than fourteen thousand dollars in goods for the store. Prices ranged from fifty cents for a pair of glasses to twenty dollars for a beaver coat. Violin strings could be purchased for fifty cents while a spittoon cost forty-four cents.

Pinson sat on the Mobile and Ohio Railroad. By 1876, two hundred people lived there. Included in the town were two dry goods stores, two grocery stores, two saloons, one drug store, a blacksmith and wagon shop, one hotel, one Masonic hall, two churches, one high school with three teachers and seventy-five pupils, three carpenters, two physicians, and two grist mills.

Two and one-half miles east of Pinson are the Pinson Indian Mounds. The site sits on a natural bluff of the south fork of the Forked Deer River. The land had been acquired from the Chickasaw Indians in the treaty of 1818. This land, known as the western territory, was then part of North Carolina. Lands in West Tennessee were given to North Carolina Revolutionary War veterans. Many of these veterans died without heirs and the grants were reacquired by the state. Colonel Thomas Henderson of Raleigh, North Carolina, was employed to search out and survey these claims. For his work he was paid a percentage of the land.

Henderson organized a surveying party, which began work on April 24, 1820; it started at Reynoldsburg on the Tennessee River and moved west. It was this surveying party who would be the first white men to find the mounds, some two thousand years after they were built. One of the surveyors was Memucan Hunt Howard who published his "recollections" in 1902. His dairy reads, "On emerging from the swamp of Forked Deer river about a dozen miles from Jackson, we found a bold spring and near it a mound six or seven feet high and large enough for a house, which we named Mount Pinson. We did not then know of the large mounds two or three miles farther south and persons who had seen them supposing it was these we had so named adopted the name as having been intended for them and they have borne that name since. I saw the large mound later and supposed it to be about seventy or seventy-five feet high and nearly four hundred yards in circumference. Near it was a square mound about twenty feet high, and other smaller ones, dikes, etc., abounded thereabout."

One member of the surveying party was a young man named Joel Pinson. He was so delighted with the discovery that the mound was named for him by the other members of the group. The mounds gained notoriety through the interest of J. G. Cisco, editor of a Jackson newspaper the *Forked Deer Blade*. (Because of his efforts, the site was also named "The City of Cisco.") From 1917 to 1919 William E. Meyers, a Smithsonian Museum archaeologist, mapped and tested the site. In the 1960s, a group of Jackson citizens succeeded in having the area purchased as a state park. The group was composed of Dr. John Nuckolls, Seale Johnson,

Saul's Mound at Pinson.

Judges Tip Taylor, Leroy Pope, and Walter Baker Harris, and college student Harbert Alexander. Forty thousand dollars was allocated for land purchase and ten thousand dollars for development. The area was declared a state park in 1967 and placed on the National Register of Historic Places in 1981.

Pinson Mounds is the largest Middle Woodland period mound group in the United States and dates from 200 B.C. to 500 A.D. The seventeen mounds and geometric earthworks served as a ceremonial site while a few of the smaller mounds held burials. The site covers more than four hundred acres. Most of the flat-topped mounds were laid out according to a master plan. Saul's Mound, the tallest mound at seventy-two feet, stands in the center of the complex. (Saul's Mound is the second largest mound in the United States!) Mounds 28 and 29, to the east of Saul's Mound, mark the northeast and southeast corners of the complex and are exactly 3,350 feet from Saul's Mound, suggesting that their positioning signified a specific purpose. Surrounding Mound 29 is a geometric embankment that was originally circular. This positioning demonstrates the builders' knowledge of basic geometry. Ozier Mound marks another corner of the mounds complex. The second tallest flat-topped mound was also a ceremonial mound. An access ramp exists on the northeast side of the mound.

Only three of the mounds are burial mounds, the largest of which are the Twin Mounds—a pair of interesting conical mounds about twenty-three feet tall. In 1983, the northern Twin Mound was excavated and determined to be built about A.D. 100. Several log tombs containing the remains of sixteen individuals were discovered. Several artifacts were found including fresh water pearls and beads, a sheet of mica, and rattles made from human skull bones. A number of cremation and activity areas have been found nearby. Rather than a village, Pinson was a ceremonial center. Based on a variety of pottery types found at the site, it appears that individuals from as far away as southern Georgia and Louisiana participated in rituals there.

Built to replicate a mound, the museum houses artifacts in a forty-five hundred square-foot exhibit area, park offices, an archaeological library, an eighty-seat theater, and the West Tennessee Regional Archaeology Office. A thirty-two-person group camp is also available. There are about six miles of trails including a nature trail and board-walk, picnic areas, and pavilions. Most trails are accessible to bikes and wheelchairs. Today Pinson Mounds is one of our most visited state parks. Nearby, the town of Pinson remains one of our quaint Madison County villages.

GHOST TOWN
ON THE HATCHIE

Hatchie Bottoms can be a lonesome place. It is primarily timber country—big timber country that borders the Hatchie River. Most of it is low lying with sloughs and oxbow lakes with the river meandering through it. The Hatchie River is West Tennessee's only unchannelized river following its original course from North Mississippi to where it enters the Mississippi River near Memphis. If you are a deer or duck hunter in that bottom, a compass is as necessary as a gun. In today's civilized world it is a quiet haven. Most days, you never see another human being—only animals. Perhaps the fear of giant cottonmouth snakes or the dread of getting lost keeps some people away. Others love its solitude.

Long ago, a town once sat on the riverbank at Estanaula Landing. (Estanaula is a Cherokee word that translates to "we cross here.") Old Hatchie Town near Bolivar and Estanaula Landing were shallow places where the river could be crossed. And for this reason, early West Tennessee towns sprang up in both places. Estanaula Landing could be found just outside of Madison County, lying on the edge of Haywood County. It was located six

Estanaula Landing.

miles from Mercer and eight miles from Denmark. To reach
it today, you would travel west on Interstate 40, exiting on
the Providence Road Exit. Then travel south on Highway
138 through Bond's Crossing until you reach the Madison
Farmers Co-Op. Then procede off to the right on Estanaula
Road which soon intersects with another gravel road and
takes you across Big Black Creek to the river where the
Tennessee Wildlife Resources Agency has built a boat
ramp. Just before you reach the river, you cross through the
site of the town. No trace of it exists today—only two
hunting camps are there to mark the site. But a parade of
historic figures once called it home.

    In the days of river commerce, it was an important ship-
ping point. In addition, Bob Wilson operated a ferryboat
there where stagecoaches could cross and continue on to
Memphis. Sometimes farmers hauled their wagons, filled
with cotton, to Memphis. But more often than not, they
brought it to Estanaula where it was stored in a warehouse

owned by Mr. Bumpus before being shipped by boat to Memphis. While at the landing they could buy groceries and stay at a hotel operated by Archie McBride.

Homes sprung up around the landing. One of the finest homes in the territory was built here by Bob Wilson, the ferryboat owner. The house had high-ceiling rooms with marble baskets of flowers hanging from the ceilings. A large basement served as a kitchen and dining room. Construction of the house was rushed by promising a quart of whiskey per man per day. Work went so quickly that by the end of the project, workers were receiving a gallon of whiskey per man per day. (Can you imagine the chaos that would occur in one of Jackson's new subdivisions if such practices still existed!)

The river could be rough depending on its height, and mishaps often occurred. One such tragedy happened at the landing when a ferryboat sank and ten-year-old twin boys, George and Louis Ford, drowned. The boys were buried in brick enclosed graves in the Old Baptist Cemetery. Tradition says that a bank robber buried thirty thousand dollars between the graves, which was stolen from a Brownsville Bank. (Apparently the story had some truth to it, as rumors say the money was dug up in the 1920s!)

Because of its remote location, the town became a haven for robbers and highwaymen. John A. Murrell, Jackson's most notorious criminal, often came here. It was here that Virgil Stewart, an informer, met Murrell and began a journey that led to Murrell's capture and imprisonment. It was also here that one of Jesse James's gangs came to camp each year until things "cooled off." Fielding Hurst, the Yankee colonel from Bethel Springs, used it as a base. (Hurst is best remembered for holding Jackson until five thousand dollars in ransom was paid. Hurst then burned most of downtown Jackson.)

During the Civil War Egbert Osborne, a preacher, was captured nearby by Federal soldiers. Held as a spy, he was threatened with execution until he saved himself by preaching "Son of Man, shall these dry bones live again" from Isaiah.

Throughout the summer of 1862, soldiers of the Twentieth and Thirtieth Illinois Infantries camped there before moving to the Battle of Britton Lane near Denmark. With hordes of mosquitoes and deer flies, life was miserable at best. Three Federal soldiers got lost in a canebrake for several days. One of the soldiers became so frightened, he killed himself. Today there is no trace of that village in the silent fields. Only a strong imagination and a sense of history can bring back the memories of Estanaula.

ELECTION
HIGH JINKS

Much of our history centers around political candidates and their election campaigns. Perhaps Madison County's consummate politician was on center stage here more than one hundred and seventy-three years ago. His name was David Crockett. Crockett first entered West Tennessee politics in 1823, when he came here from Middle Tennessee. Prior to coming here, he served as a member of the state legislature, having been elected in 1821.

Despite modern day television conceptions, Crockett was a hard-working, astute politician who represented the common man. His father was a Revolutionary War veteran and his mother was a sister-in-law of Governor John Sevier. For twelve years he championed the Whig Party throughout West Tennessee. During this period he served as a major irritant for Andrew Jackson—the man who represented the Democratic Party in Tennessee. Andrew Jackson felt very close to the city named for him. His sister-in-law, Jane Hays, lived here and had three daughters and two sons. Thus Jackson had three nieces and two nephews here, all of whom were instrumental in the development of Jackson.

One of the nieces married Dr. William Butler, who is called the father of the city of Jackson. Butler was responsible for the location of Jackson. He was Jackson's most prominent citizen. In 1823 Crockett opposed him in the race for the state legislature. Quiet and well educated, Butler had his hands full with the colorful Crockett. At a dinner at Dr. Butler's home, Crockett was startled to find a beautiful rug on the floor. Unused to such things, Crockett refused to step on it. Instead he backed up and ran and jumped over it. Later he would describe the experience to prospective voters by saying, "Why my fellow citizens, my wealthy competitor walks every day on 'store goods' finer than any your wives or daughters ever wore."

Crockett's best trick occurred while traveling throughout the territory speaking "on the stump" against Dr. Butler. In those days, it was the custom for competing political candidates to debate throughout the district. These events were well attended with large amounts of home cooked food and corn whiskey. Often candidates would speak from one to two hours. Dr. Butler had been speaking first with Crockett following. But on one occasion, Butler let Crockett go first. It was a great mistake. With a twinkle in his eye, Crockett began with "My fellow citizens," and then proceeded to give Dr. Butler's speech word for word. Butler was left speechless for Crockett had already given his speech! When election day came, Crockett was elected. In all probability, Dr. Butler was too aristocratic to win an election like this. But in later years, he would have his revenge by placing the entire Jackson machine against Crockett.

In 1826 Crockett sought the twelfth Congressional seat in the United States House of Representatives. His opponent was Adam Rankin Alexander, a United States surveyor. Alexander had settled with three other individuals on the bank of the Forked Deer River in 1820 where the present day site of the West Tennessee Experiment Station is located. Crockett rolled up a majority of 2,784 votes, winning easily, and was on his way to Washington. Crockett's success, first in Nashville then in Washington, would become intolerable to Andrew Jackson. As a result, Jackson came here in 1825 to champion the Democratic party.

In 1829 Crockett was opposed by William Fitzgerald of Weakley County. Crockett cried foul when a legislative gerrymandering of the district occurred. Despite this, Crockett won and returned to Washington. Fitzgerald managed to defeat Crockett in 1831, but lost to him again in 1833. Lurking in the background during this period was an individual named Adam Huntsman. One of our first settlers, Huntsman had come to Madison County in 1821. He built his residence in the Cotton Gin Grove Community. (His home site is adjacent to the F.O.P. Lodge on Cotton Grove Road.) Huntsman was nicknamed "Peg Leg," having lost a leg in the Creek Indian War. Also sporting a hair piece and false teeth, he was one of Jackson's first lawyers and county commissioners.

Huntsman represented Madison, Hardeman, Haywood, Fayette, Tipton, and Shelby Counties in the state senate for two terms from 1831–1835. His rivalry with Crockett began in 1828 when citizens urged him to run against the incumbent. Aware of Crockett's popularity, Huntsman declined to run. In 1831, Crockett publicly broke with Andrew Jackson, president of the United States! Crockett stated that Jackson's followers reminded him of large dogs with collars that had Jackson's name on them as owner. It was a risky statement. Huntsman continued to poke fun at Crockett, writing satirical editorials in local newspapers describing him as a lost horse.

In 1835 Huntsman finally came out to run against Crockett in a fun-filled campaign across the Western District. Perhaps the high point of the election occurred when the two were traveling together, speaking on the stump for hours at a time. Staying together at a prominent Democratic farmer's home, they shared the same bed. Waiting until Huntsman was asleep, Crockett crept through the darkened house to the room where the farmer's daughter slept. Hearing a scratching noise on her door, the young woman woke up screaming. Crockett then went back to his bedroom, stomping a wooden chair leg on the floor. The sound was exactly like the noise Adam Huntsman's peg leg would have made. The farmer was furious and threatened to kill him. Only Crockett's interference saved him, but the story circulated through the district to the delight of Crockett's supporters. Election day found Huntsman winning the election by a narrow margin of 4,652 votes to 4,400.

Crockett was furious with the outcome and again cried foul. He claimed that President Jackson used his "franking" privilege to flood West Tennessee with material against him. He also claimed that the Union Bank in Jackson paid twenty-five dollars a vote for Huntsman, a princely sum in those days. There would be no contested election however. Crockett, in a foul mood, marched to the steps of the courthouse where he snarled at his supporters telling them, "You can go to hell, for I am going to Texas." It was a great mistake, for Crockett would be killed eight months later defending the Alamo.

Huntsman continued to be active in politics until his death in 1849. He is buried in Old Salem Cemetery on Cotton Grove Road with all three of his wives. Prominent in many fields, he is best remembered for his defeat of Crockett.

Adam Huntsman's Marker—Old Salem Cemetery.

RIVERSIDE
Our Oldest Cemetery

After Jackson was organized in 1822, the little village soon felt the need for a cemetery. The first cemetery for the citizens of Jackson was located in a chestnut grove on a small rise of ground along the northeast side of what is now Johnson Street near its intersection with Airways. Some thirty to forty people were buried there before the cemetery was abandoned and forgotten. When a brickyard was established on the site, the old graves were discovered and the remains moved to Riverside Cemetery. One of the graves moved to Riverside Cemetery was that of Colonel John H. Gibson, a local hero of the War of 1812. Another body moved to Riverside was that of Mrs. Thomas Shannon, whose remains were identified by a comb in her hair.

Riverside Cemetery is a historic ten-acre burial ground located on the southeast corner of Riverside Drive and Sycamore Street. The cemetery was established in 1824 on one acre of ground donated by Samuel Shannon. Shortly thereafter Samuel Lancaster acquired about four acres of land adjacent to the cemetery and began to sell burial plots. Soon after the Civil War, the city purchased land on the north side of the cemetery from the estate of James Caruthers. For years this portion was called the Caruthers Division. With the rapid growth of the railroads bringing in more people, the city felt the need for additional cemetery space. In 1878, the city purchased land on the north side from Thomas L. Robinson.

For years this burial ground was known as the "city cemetery." In the spring of 1878 a contest was held to name it. Benjamin Davidson submitted the name "Riverside" because of its close proximity to the south fork of the Forked Deer River. In a newspaper editorial dated May 8, 1879, this name was deemed as the most fitting suggestion. The name continues today.

By the mid-1880s Riverside was becoming crowded, which prompted the beginning of two new cemeteries. City officials helped black citizens to begin Mt. Olivet Cemetery on West Forrest Avenue. A group of private citizens established another cemetery west of town, known as Hollywood Cemetery.

For sixty years Riverside served as Jackson's primary cemetery. Most of our early settlers and founding fathers are buried there. The first burial was in September 1824 when Mary Jane Butler, the daughter of Dr. William E. Butler, was interred there. (Butler is considered to be "the father of Jackson.") This burial in 1824 makes Riverside our oldest cemetery, since the oldest marker in Old Salem Cemetery on Cotton Grove Road is dated 1825.

The Riverside Cemetery Improvement Association was organized in 1918 to preserve and maintain the grounds. This lasted until 1976 when the city assumed the responsibility. Today the grounds are beautifully kept as a memorial to our earliest Jacksonians.

Through the gate toward the northeast corner of the cemetery is a thin broken stone that marks the grave of W. H. Conner. In 1881 Conner refused to let his daughter marry. In an ensuing argument with the prospective groom, Conner was shot and killed. Next are the graves of Eddie and Willie

Harkens, six- and eight-year-old brothers. In 1889, they were playing with two other boys in a sand ditch on Stoddert Street when the bank collapsed, killing all four. In the far back left corner is the marker for E. F. Neill, a prosperous and well-liked merchant. Neill fell on hard times and shot himself in 1885.

The monument for Dr. William E. Butler can be found on Third Street. Having come to Jackson in 1819 following the Chickasaw Treaty, Butler returned with his family in 1821. He was married to Patsy Thompson Hays, a niece of Andrew Jackson. Butler's life reads like a novel and includes adventures such as serving with Jackson at the Battle of New Orleans and running against David Crockett for a seat in the state legislature. Butler owned a race track near the site of today's Chamber of Commerce building, which he later donated to the Memphis Conference Female Institute, the predecessor of Lambuth University. In addition, he owned the corner lot where the First American Bank was located, before it was destroyed to make way for the new City Hall. Butler was buried in Riverside in 1882.

On Fourth Street is the grave of Rudolph Hafeli, a railroad engineer who set a record by pulling one hundred fifty freight cars. A few weeks later he was killed when he hit a cow, causing the train to leave the tracks. Hafeli jumped from the wreck but was killed when a car load of cotton bales fell on him. No one else was injured. If only a song had been written about him, Jackson would have had two famous engineers.

The first marker in the middle of Fourth Street is that of Miss Mary Timberlake, one of Jackson's leading socialites and society members of the 1890s. Further down the street just past a marble angel is the tombstone of J. W. McClaren, a Jackson physician. During World War I in Europe, he observed the Red Cross and its work there. Upon his return to Jackson he started our first chapter of the American Red Cross.

Riverside Cemetery.

Going west up Fifth Street stands a tall monument of William Dunaway, a Methodist minister and early mayor. (Most of Jackson's mayors are buried in Riverside). Re–elected in 1872, he died before taking office. Further on to the left is the Reavis family plot. James Reavis was a dentist, shoe maker, and city marshall. His son ran a tinsmith shop. (Look closely at the front of Nando Jones's store at 111 West Lafayette Street where you can still read "Reavis and Sons Tinsmiths.") At the end of the plot is the marker for Reavis's son-in-law, Tom Gaston. Gaston was one of the most colorful individuals in Jackson's history, and our most famous chief of police. He died in February 1918. Just ahead is a tall flat stone with a Tennessee flag engraved on it. This nearly unreadable stone marks the grave of J. H. Williams, a local constable who died in 1878. After being declared dead and his head wrapped up for burial, he recovered consciousness and lived for eight more hours! Turning left and going south on Sixth Street is the grave of Thomas Henderson who died in 1877. Henderson served under Nathan Bedford Forrest in the Civil War and commanded a company of scouts, known simply as Henderson's Scouts.

Nearby is another marker. This one indicates the burial place of Barney Frye, who reportedly shot himself in 1880. Because of a stormy marriage, rumors persisted that his wife shot him. As if to dispute the rumors, his wife had "Erected By His Wife" engraved on his marker. Next are the markers for John and Mary Bond. They are best known for Mary's brother Robert Cartmell, who is buried to the southeast across Seventh Street. Another brother lost an eye in the Battle of Shiloh. Surviving the war, he lived in Jackson until he was run over by a car in 1913! (It must have come from his blind side.)

Going down Seventh Street is the burial place of Dr. T. K. Ballard, the Madison County coroner for many years. This is one of the few recent burials in Riverside. To the right of Dr. Ballard is a tall pink granite stone marking the grave of D. H. "Ham" King. King was one of our most famous mayors and also served as fire chief in the 1870s. He owned and operated a saloon known as King's Palace Saloon. For years it was Jackson's most prestigious saloon and gathering place for political hopefuls from across the state. To the right of King is the grave of Job Umphlett, a partner in Umphlett and Robertson Furniture and Undertaking. Later it became Umphlett and Griffin, known today as Griffin Funeral Home.

On Eighth Street is the Stoddert family plot. Lieutenant Thomas Ewell is probably buried in this plot. Ewell was a member of the Second Tennessee Volunteers in the Mexican War and was in the Battle of Cerro Gordo against Mexican General Santa Anna. Only twenty-three, he was mortally wounded and died soon after the battle. His body was brought back to Jackson in a sealed coffin to be placed at Riverside.

Continuing across toward Eighth Street is the first of two McCorry plots. The McCorrys were one of Jackson's earliest Catholic families. Judge Henry McCorry was considered to be among Tennessee's most powerful Democrats in the late 1800s. Even today he is remembered for his efforts in getting the votes recounted in an election where a Republican had been elected as governor. When the votes were counted a second time, the Democratic candidate had the most votes and Judge McCorry was given credit for "stealing" the election. Musidora McCorry is also buried in the family plot. The Jackson chapter of the United Daughters of the Confederacy is named for her. Tradition says that Henry McCorry, along with Middleton Hays, started Jackson's chapter of the Ku Klux Klan shortly after the end of the war. The robes for the Klansmen were made by Musidora McCorry with the help of her sisters Ellen and Pet.

On Eighth Street, looking toward the back, lies the oldest part of the cemetery. An odd shaped marker with shoulders marks the grave of Elijah Bigelow. A native of

Massachusetts, he was an attorney and the editor of Jackson's first newspaper, the *Jackson Gazette*. Bigelow and his wife started the first school in Jackson. Further back is one of several of the Hays's lots located in the cemetery. There is the marker for Richard Jackson Hays, the first mayor of Jackson from 1845 to May 1846, who resigned to fight in the Mexican War. Returning from the war, he was again elected mayor in 1856 and for a third time in 1858.

Also located on the Eighth Street side of the cemetery is the marker for Brigadier General Alexander W. Campbell. General Campbell was the son of J. W. Campbell, Jackson's first banker and insurance agent. An attorney before the war, he led the Thirty-third Tennessee Infantry at Shiloh where he was severely wounded. In 1864 he was captured at Lexington, Tennessee, and sent to a federal prison. Paroled in 1865, he was promoted to Brigadier General, and served under Nathan Bedford Forrest until the end of the war. He resumed his law practice after the war and also served as president of the M and O Railroad. Becoming interested in politics in 1880, he was unsuccessful in seeking the Democratic nomination for governor. He died in 1893. Nearby is the grave of his daughter Kate Campbell Robertson. She was an early president of the National Congress of Mothers, later to become the national Parent-Teacher Association (PTA). In her honor, one of her sons donated land to the city, which was named Kate Campbell Robertson Park. When the last of the Robertson clan died five years ago, the family left more than four million dollars to Jackson charities!

To the left is the grave of Colonel Robert I. Chester who was married to Elizabeth Hays, another daughter of Jane Donelson Hays. Chester thus married a niece of Andrew Jackson and became the brother-in-law of Dr. William E. Butler. He served under Jackson as quartermaster of the Third Tennessee Regiment in the War of 1812. Moving to Jackson, he was a merchant, postmaster

(1825–1833), United States marshall under Presidents Taylor and Pierce, and later a partner in a lumber business and steam mill on Reelfoot Lake. Chester County is named for him.

Nearby on the south slope lie the graves of seventy-five Confederate soldiers. Another forty lie close by. The identities of all but two of these are unknown. Two Union soldiers are also buried here. In the years following the war, the ladies of Jackson would come here on May 15 to lay flowers on the graves. (This date marked the mustering in date of Jackson's Sixth Tennessee Infantry.) This custom spread across the South and became known as "Decoration Day." Known today as Memorial Day it is celebrated across the nation on the last Monday in May to commemorate the American dead in all wars. (Despite local custom, Waterloo, New York, is considered to be the first place this took place in 1866.)

Nearby are two tall mouments for James Dixon McClellan and his wife, Isabella. James was an early West Tennessee attorney from a promient family. He was an influential member of Bascom Chapel Methodist Church (this church no longer exists). McClellan Road is named for him.

To the right is the Cartmell family plot. Robert Cartmell, Jackson's most famous diarist, is buried here with his wife, Jane. On the side of their marker is a tribute to Robert's brother William who was killed in the Battle of Perryville. Beyond and to the right of the Cartmells is a tall marker for Captain Joseph Freeman, an officer of the Jackson Grays, a company of the Sixth Tennessee Infantry who died at Shiloh. Another officer of that unit, Lieutenant Ike Jackson, was also killed at Shiloh and is buried in Riverside. (Of the twelve hundred men in the Sixth Tennessee, more than five hundred were killed, wounded, or missing after the two-day battle.) Moving ahead near a dogwood tree is a tombstone marked Ned and Becca. These are two of the few slave burial sites still marked. There are others but their wooden markers have long since vanished. Also on the south slopes are the graves of Jackson's paupers who are buried by the city. (Riverside is the only cemetery maintained by the city of Jackson, which gives them a place to bring indigents with no family.)

6

JACKSON'S HANGING GROUNDS

ecent newspaper and television reports are full of stories of a Cuban inmate in Florida. Convicted of murder, he was sentenced to be electrocuted in Florida's famous electric chair. When the electricity was turned on, the charge was so severe that the prisoner's leather mask caught on fire. Needless to say, he was pronounced dead shortly thereafter. One can only imagine the uproar that would have caused should the execution have occurred in Jackson!

In Jackson's early years, convicted criminals were quickly and often severely punished. Within two years of Jackson's founding, a courthouse and a jail were constructed. In contrast to the cost of Jackson's new city hall and jail costs, it is interesting to note what those buildings cost in 1823. Construction cost of the courthouse was $135, and the jail cost $95!

On January 2, 1823, Jackson's first Board of Commissioners passed the following laws:

1. Any person or persons found guilty of disorderly or riotous conduct within the limits of the Corporation shall forfeit and pay $5.

2. Any Person or persons, putting or attempting to put any stud horse or Jack to a Mare or exhibiting the same to public square or streets or alleys of the Town shall for each offense forfeit and pay $5.

3. All Peddlers and Showmen shall before they proceed to sell or exhibit, as the case may be, pay $10 license to do so which shall be good for the month, at the expiration of which time said license must be renewed at the rates of $10 per month so long as they may continue to sell, exhibit, in the Town of Jackson—and any failure to procure said license as aforesaid they and each of them shall forfeit and pay $50, for each offense.

4. Any person or persons who shall run a horse race or run a horse at full speed within the incorporation limits of said Town, shall forfeit and pay the sum of $20 for each offense.

5. Any person or persons who shall shoot a Gun or Pistol within said Town, shall forfeit and pay the sum of $20 for each offense.

6. Any person or persons who shall be found guilty of the mischievous and dangerous practice of fastening matches or other combustible substances to dogs or other animals, within said Town shall forfeit and pay $5 for each offense.

7. It shall hereafter be the duty of Merchants and every other person who may wish to retail Goods, Wares, or Merchandise within said Town, to procure a license first; which shall be good and sufficient for the term of one year from and after date thereof. Provided nevertheless, that no Merchant or other person shall be entitled to receive such license without previously paying into the hands of the proper officer the sum of $12.50 and every Merchant or other person who shall violate this law shall forfeit and pay the sum of $25.

8. No person or persons shall retail spirituous liquors within said Town without first procuring a license

from the proper authority which said license shall be good and sufficient authority to such person or persons for the term of one year. Provided nevertheless, that no person shall be entitled to receive said license without first paying twelve dollars and fifty cents. And any person selling or retailing spirituous liquors without a license shall forfeit and pay $25.

9. Each lot in the Town of Jackson is hereby subjected to an annual tax of one half per centrum ad valorem, agreeably to the original price given for said Lot—to be collected by the Town Constable for the present year so soon as practicable.

10. Any person or persons who shall be found guilty of playing cards, Dice, or any other game of Hazard or Address within the incorporated limit of said town shall forfeit and pay $10 for each offense.

11. Any Inn or Tavern Keeper or Keepers of any Ordinary who shall suffer any game of Hazard or Address to be played in their house or houses shall forfeit and pay $25 for each offense.

12. It shall be the duty of the Town Constable from time to time to cause to be removed all nuisances from said Town. The expense of which shall be charged to the person or persons who may have caused or erected the same, for which services the Board of Commissioners shall make the said Constable a reasonable allowance.

13. It shall be the duty of the Town Constable to preserve good order during Public Worship in said town. And to take notice of any person or persons who may disturb those so worshipping.

14. It shall be the duty of the secretary of said Board of Commissioners to issue license to any person applying for the same. Provided said person may be entitled to the same by the authority of the foregoing BY-LAWS and for every license so issued the said Secretary shall be entitled to receive the sum of Fifty cents, from the person applying for the same.

Though Jackson was a frontier town, it is obvious that the city fathers intended for it to be a peaceful place. Crimes of a serious nature were dealt with more severely. Horse thieves like John Murrell, Jackson's most notorious criminal, were branded with the letters HT on their thumbs. Jackson had its own public whipping posts where crowds gathered to watch the prisoner being lashed. Jackson also had a public pillory, which was a wooden framework erected on a post with holes through which a person's hands and head were placed. Bystanders could then laugh at and taunt the prisoner.

Frontier Jacksonians did not have many of the forms of entertainment we are blessed with today. It will probably come as a shock that one of the most popular events was to witness a public hanging. Jackson's "hanging grounds" were located on Airways just west of the Gulf, Mobile and Ohio Railroad station near the present site of Touchstone, Inc. On the appointed day, whole families would gather with picnic lunches and follow the procession from the jail to the gallows site. Huge crowds would visit and sing hymns until the appointed time. The hanging of a notorious criminal often turned into one of Jackson's most festive occasions. Large crowds would gather for the event, sometimes numbering more than a thousand people.

One of the most interesting hangings occurred in 1849 when a convicted murderer named John M. Riley was sentenced to be hanged. The criminal had been convicted of murder after he confessed while intoxicated and denied it when he became sober.

Although Riley had been convicted of the crime, he still maintained that he was innocent and prayed that the Lord would save him by some sign from heaven. The gallows were prepared and the rope was about to be placed on his neck when a terrible storm arose, seeming to come from nowhere. The crowd dispersed with Riley left standing on the gallows. When the storm abated, the crowd returned

and the hanging took place. Obviously, neither the crowd
nor the hangman believed in signs from heaven. Years later
a man on his death bed in Obion County confessed to the
crime for which Riley had been hanged!

In 1875 Milton McLean was convicted of the murder of
Thaddeus Pope and sentenced to be hanged on January 7,
1876. Fascinated with the dignity and bravery of the prisoner, an immense crowd gathered to witness the event. The
gallows had been erected near the banks of the Forked Deer
River about one-half mile south of the courthouse. Friends
gathered to call on the prisoner, and various ministers tried

Hanging gallows.

to get him to profess religion. He remained aloof and indifferent to their efforts. When the hour came, the prisoner dressed in a neat black suit, left the jail, mounted the waiting wagon, and seated himself between two ministers on his coffin.

One of Jackson's most famous mayors, Ham King, along with the sheriff and a group of guards and the entire police force mounted their horses and formed a circle around the prisoner. Arriving at the hanging grounds, McLean climbed up on the scaffold and astonished everyone by having a conversation with Sam Brown, the carpenter who had built the scaffold. "Sam, I hope you have done a good job of it." To which the carpenter replied, "I have done my best." Following scripture and prayer, the sheriff read the sentence and asked the prisoner if he had anything to say. "Nothing" was his reply. The crowd then sang a familiar hymn, "There Is a Fountain Filled with Blood." After a ten minute wait, a black hood was placed over McLean's head and the trap door was dropped. Death by strangulation took twenty-five minutes!

More than one hundred years later, convicted criminals in Tennessee are rarely executed. Only one has been executed in recent years. That execution was very different from those of long ago.

7

WE COULD HAVE BEEN KITTY HAWK

Who would believe that Jackson almost replaced Kitty Hawk, North Carolina, as the birthplace of the airplane. Strange—but true!

In 1858, three years before the beginning of the Civil War an eccentric professor from Spring Creek tried to get a patent for a flying machine. The professor's name was Isham Walker. The flying machine was named the "Giant Trout." The machine was huge. It consisted of three mammoth balloons forty-five feet wide and seventy feet high. It was held together with wire and sheet copper and coated inside and out with India rubber. Two of the balloons were side by side with the third one forward and below. Gas was in the top balloons and the bottom one was a cabin where two engines were mounted capable of five hundred revolutions per minute. It was designed to travel at speeds exceeding three hundred miles per hour at a height of more than two miles from the earth's surface.

Walker asked Congress for an appropriation of a million dollars to purchase materials and two thousand dollars a year for superintending construction, or for a lifetime salary of five thousand dollars a year if he turned over all

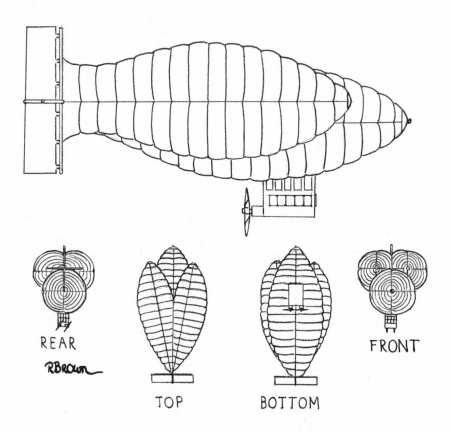

REAR

R.Brown

TOP   BOTTOM   FRONT

The Giant Trout.

patent rights to the government. Congress refused, other investors declined, and Walker never got his ship airborne.

Imagine if Walker had succeeded—driving through downtown Jackson in your horse and buggy and looking up to see something resembling a blimp passing over the courthouse two miles up in the clouds? If Albert Sidney Johnson could have flown over the battlefield at Shiloh, he would have been able to see General Don Carlos Buell's Army of the Ohio arriving at Pittsburg Landing to reinforce General Grant, and thus ordered the Confederate force to keep on attacking. Nathan Bedford Forrest would certainly have looked different commanding his troops from the Giant Trout rather than on horseback.

Jackson also lost another chance to become famous for the invention of the airplane. F. E. Earnshaw built an airplane along the same line as the model pioneered by the Wright Brothers. The engine was too heavy for the aircraft and his experiment was not successful. This occurred some three years prior to the Wright Brothers' successful flight from the sand dunes along the outer banks of North Carolina.

Through the persistence of Judge Milton Brown and later I. B. Tigrett, Jackson's early industrial growth and prominence would come with the arrival of the railroads, rather than through the invention of airplanes. Both Professor Isham Walker and F. E. Earnshaw are long gone and for the most part forgotten. However, if either of their two inventions had been successful, it would have certainly changed our history!

8

OUR MOST FAMOUS OUTLAW

As far as criminals go, no one can compare to John A. Murrell. Emma Inman Williams, in *Historic Madison*, referred to him as the "western land pirate." Another writer called him a satanic outlaw preacher. You can find him on the Internet listed as John A. Murrell, "The Reverend Devil." Could someone born almost two hundred years ago have been this bad? Apparently so!

Murrell was born in Virginia in 1804. His family moved to Columbia, Tennessee, shortly after his birth. His father was an innkeeper and also a Methodist minister who traveled the gospel district. His mother was quite different—she "learnt" him and all of her children to steal as soon as they could walk, so that by the time he became of age he was a "confirmed evil doer and formally adopted robbery as a profession."

Murrell's name first appears in the court records of Williamson County, Tennessee, in 1823 when he was fined fifty dollars for fighting. Two years later he was back in court, this time for gambling. Shortly thereafter he was charged with stealing a horse from a widow in Williamson County. He was tried in Nashville where he was found guilty. As punishment he was whipped until his back was bloody, branded H. T. (horsethief) on his thumbs, and sentenced to twelve months in prison. A small boy who witnessed the branding recalled the scene in the crowded courtroom.

The judge was seated on a high seat surrounded by a hand railing, and the prisoner's box nearby. John Murrell, handsomely dressed but quite unconcerned, was conducted to the prisoner's box, instructed to lay his hand on the railing while the sheriff took from his pocket a piece of new hemp and bound Murrell's hand securely to the railing. In a short while a big Negro named Jeffry came in bringing a tinner's stove that looked like a lantern and placed it on the floor. Being anxious to see all that was going on, I climbed upon the railing close to Murrell. Mr. Horton, the sheriff, took from the little stove the branding iron, a long instrument, which looked very much like the soldering irons now used by tinners. He looked at the iron, which was red-hot and then put it on Murrell's hand. The skin fried like meat. Mr. Horton held it there until the smoke rose probably two feet when he removed the iron. Mr. Horton then untied Murrell's hand. Murrell, who had up to this time never moved, produced a white handkerchief and wiped his hand several times. It was all over, and the sheriff took Murrell back to jail where he was yet to suffer punishment by being whipped and placed in the pillory.

Although Murrell operated in seven or eight states, he made Madison County his home near Denmark, where he studied criminal law in order to avoid its dangers. He also learned to preach revivalist type sermons. While he preached, his associates would steal the horses outside of the church. One such incident occurred at the Presbyterian Church in Denmark where the disgruntled churchgoers had to walk home after church. Apparently

John Murrell.

he did not preach on the eighth commandment about stealing!

Most of the stolen horses were kept in a corral near Hickman, Kentucky, until they could be brought back to West Tennessee and sold. He made big money stealing slaves, telling each one of his plan to resell them three or four times, and then divide the money with them and let them escape to the free North. When the slave became too well known, that is after he had been stolen and resold several times and too many advertisements appeared in the newspapers for him, then Murrell would select some quiet spot on a lonely road, kill the slave, "debowel him," fill the cavity with rocks, and dump him into some convenient stream. It seemed that the secret of the desperado's success was his thoroughness with which he destroyed condemning evidence.

Another hiding place for stolen slaves and horses was in a canebreak in Arkansas on the Mississippi River. His gang of thieves was known as the Clan of the Mystic Confederacy. Some accounts place as many as one thousand members in his group. Whether true or not, contemporary sources tell of a plan to lead a slave revolt and take over the city of New Orleans and later Mississippi and Louisiana. The date of the rebellion was set for Christmas Day, 1835. Before this could happen he was captured in Florence, Alabama. He was sent to Brownsville and then was tried in Jackson in July and August, 1834. Though charged with stealing and murder, he was only convicted of stealing slaves. He was sentenced to ten years of hard labor at the state penitentiary in Nashville. Upon being discharged in April 1844, he then went to Pikesville in Bledsoe County and became a blacksmith for a short time before he died.

Through the years, the story of John Murrell continues to grow. Even today treasure hunters search for caches of buried gold. One such treasure is rumored to lie beneath a fake cemetery, complete with an iron fence and fake tomb-stones. To date it has not been found. It is improbable that Murrell committed all of the crimes he was credited with, but truth or fiction, he is our most famous outlaw! Murrell's historical marker is on Airways near the entrance to the airport.

JACKSON'S MISSING GENERAL

ew people, including the author, had heard of Alexander Blackburn Bradford until recently. However, Bradford led a fascinating life history that is outlined below. It all started with a letter in late May, 2000, from Bradford's great-great-great grandson, J. Bradford Williamson in Miami, Florida, who was looking for the general's grave. I called him, and he responded with pictures and the life story of General Bradford. What follows is a history of his life and the search for his burial plot.

Bradford was born in Jefferson County, Tennessee, on June 2, 1799. He was the son of Benjamin and Mary Bradford, East Tennessee pioneers. Both of his grandfathers were Revolutionary War veterans. After studying law at the University of Tennessee, he served as a senate clerk under James K. Polk in the Thirteenth General Assembly of Tennessee. He was only twenty years old at the time.

In 1821 Bradford moved to Jackson, Tennessee, becoming one of our first settlers. On November 14 of that year he was admitted to the bar of the First Circuit Court of Madison County. Soon after this he was named as the first district attorney, at that time called solicitor general, for the Western District of Tennessee.

In 1821 Bradford married Dorthula Miller, the daughter of Pleasant and Mary Louisa Blount Miller. Pleasant Miller was one of Jackson's most prominent lawyers and later served as chancellor for the new Chancery Court of West Tennessee. Mary Louisa was the daughter of William Blount, governor of the Southwest Territory. Another daughter married Colonel William H. Stephens who was the commander of the Sixth Tennessee Infantry (CSA), a West Tennessee regiment that included many Jackson soldiers. (Stephens was famous for his involvement in national politics against presidential candidate James Buchanan.) Bradford's marriage lasted fifteen years before Dorthula died in 1836. She is buried in Riverside Cemetery in an unmarked plot.

In 1834 Bradford served as one of two prosecuting attorneys in the trial of John A. Murrell, one of the most notorious criminals of the early southeastern United States and certainly the most famous criminal in Jackson's history. (A historical marker details his life of crime near the airport.) The trial, lasting two months, accused Murrell of murder and of stealing slaves. Acquitted of the murder charge, he was convicted of stealing slaves and sentenced to ten years in prison, which effectively ended his career of crime.

Bradford was a little man with a strong military air about him. It is said he used to pull his coat around him and strut in front of a full-length mirror, asking all comers if he didn't look remarkably like Napoleon Bonaparte. Though short in statue, Bradford was a gifted military commander. In 1831 he was elected brigadier-general of the Fourteenth Brigade, Tennessee Militia (the equivalent of today's National Guard). Two years later he was elected major general of the Western District of Tennessee.

In 1836, Osceola, Chief of the Seminole Indians, led an uprising called the Second Seminole War. In addition to the regular United States Army, a number of states, including Tennessee, sent volunteers from their militias. Bradford volunteered for the war in Florida, enlisting as a private; he was soon elected colonel.

During the Florida War, he commanded a regiment of volunteers from Tennessee. At one point the regiment expected to have a battle with the Indians. Just before the battle, General Bradford was taken sick. Some of the volunteers thought and perhaps hinted that it was very convenient to be indisposed just then. He was aware of the surmise of some of his men that he was a coward. However, in a few weeks a battle was fought by the Withlacooche River. When General Bradford had formed his regiment in line of battle, he determined to draw the enemy's fire. For this purpose he ordered a company to advance; but a moment's reflection determined him to sacrifice his own life instead of those of the company. Without saying a word he waived his hand to the company, thus ordered out to retire into line again, and drawing his sword, he galloped out in front of the enemy's line. In a moment, hundreds of rifles were leveled upon him and fired. Miraculously, he escaped unhurt. He then deliberately returned to his regiment who had watched his movement with intense anxiety. From one end of the extended line to the other arose a shout of acclamation.

Another war was fought in 1836 that was of no small interest to the people of Tennessee: the War for Texas Independence. The deaths of a number of Tennesseans during the battle of the Alamo aroused feelings of ire and sympathy in the hearts of Tennesseans everywhere; the town of Jackson was no exception. In April, 1836 (the Alamo had fallen on March 6), a rally in Jackson netted $750 in contributions for the support of the Texas cause and appointed a committee to "solicit and receive contributions of money for the purpose of arming and equipping such persons as may volunteer in the service of Texas." Alexander Bradford was a member of this committee. In addition, two companies of volunteers were raised in Madison County to

General Alexander Bradford.

rush to aid the beleaguered Texans. One of these companies, the Madison Grays, which numbered sixty-five, was commanded by Bradford. These two companies never went to Texas because soon after their organization, Sam Houston and his Texans were victorious at San Jacinto, and Tennessee Governor Cannon countermanded his call for troops. After the war, Bradford returned to Tennessee where he was elected to a term in the state senate in 1837.

In 1839 Alexander Bradford moved to Holly Springs, Mississippi, where he set up a law practice and was owner of the Holly Springs and State Line Railroad Company. He was elected to the legislature representing Marshall County, Mississippi, in 1841 and again in 1852. In 1847 he was defeated as a candidate for governor of Mississippi. In 1852 he lost a bid for the United States House of Representatives.

In 1846 the United States declared war against Mexico. Bradford volunteered for the Mississippi militia. On June 18, 1846, an election was held to determine who would be the commanding officer. Bradford received 350 votes. Jefferson Davis was next with 300 votes. Bradford refused the election stating,"No man should take command of this regiment without that full confidence." A second ballot was then held, and Davis was elected colonel by a plurality of some 147 votes out of more than 900 ballots. Bradford was appointed major and served as third in command.

During the Mexican War, Alexander B. Bradford was conspicuous for bravery. After the Battle of Monterrey, Bradford recalled, "I was in all of the fight, saw everything and was exposed fifteen hours to cannon balls, grape canister, and musketry, grazed seven times but escaped unhurt." At the Battle of Buena Vista, both Colonel McClung and Jefferson Davis had been wounded which added to their glory and publicity. This was more than the fiery little general could stand and he rushed up and down the lines, "waving his arms in the air, and exclaiming, 'My God! Can't one bullet hit me?'" Reuben

Davis stated that this was the "only case I ever heard of where a man was absolutely broken hearted because a bullet failed to hit him."

At Buena Vista, Bradford was appalled when he thought that the Mississippi Regiment was retreating. Not having heard Davis's order to retire, Bradford was reported to have called out in a most excited manner, "Shoot me! . . . Ah, kill me! The Mississippi Regiment has run and I'll be damned if I want to live another minute." Davis's order was transmitted to Bradford, and shortly thereafter the Mississippi regiment reformed and started an advance that helped to carry the day.

Jefferson Davis was highly appreciative of Alexander B. Bradford's military expertise. After Buena Vista, Davis reported: "To Major Bradford I offer my thanks for the prompt and creditable manner in which he executed all the orders I gave him, and especially refer to the delicate duty assigned him of restoring order among the files of another regiment when rendered unsteady by the fire of the enemy's artillery."

After the war Bradford returned to Holly Springs. In 1852 he moved to Bolivar County, Mississippi, where he established a plantation, Bradford Place. In 1861 he was elected to the Provisional Congress of the Confederate States of America. After his term expired, Bradford did not seek reelection but was again elected to the Mississippi legislature in 1863 and 1864 representing Bolivar County. The end of the Civil War left Bradford impoverished, but he was able to recoup some of his losses by practicing law in Bolivar County.

One of the most amusing stories of Bradford describes an unsuccessful attempt to remarry. He was a widower and proposed to a wealthy widow who refused him. Drawing himself up in all of his dignity, he exclaimed, "Madam, if you won't marry Major Bradford, who in hell will you marry?"

Bradford died in the summer of 1873. His obituary was published in the Memphis *Sunday Appeal* on July 13, 1873. In part it states that,

His later years have been passed in comparative retirement, partly with his children at Holly Springs, to whom he was almost an idol, and partly in Bolivar County, where his property is situated. General Bradford was remarkable for independence, honesty, frankness and truth. Of a strikingly handsome person and military carriage, he bore the weight of years with unbent form, and with the proud, firm step of a born soldier. His eagle eye flashed with the same fire at the age of seventy-three as when he charged the Indian hammocks in 1836, and the Mexican batteries in 1847. No reverses ever subdued him; no dangers ever appalled him. Here in his native Tennessee his fame is cherished with special fondnes. . . . By his own request his remains, at a suitable time, will be brought to Jackson, Tennessee, to be laid by the side of her who was the bright and morning-star of his youth, and among the graves of those who knew him best and loved him longest.

In May of 2000, his great-great-great grandson, J. Bradford Williamson of Miami, Florida, planned a trip to Jackson to visit Bradford's gravesite. However, there is no record of him being buried in Jackson. His wife Darthula is buried in Riverside Cemetery. Her tombstone is so weathered as to be unreadable. It is the belief that Bradford is not buried at Riverside Cemetery. In order to avoid a futile trip, Williamson visited Holly Springs instead. The curator for the Marshall County Museum in Holly Springs stated that Bradford's body was brought by wagon from Bolivar County to Holly Springs where he was buried at the Hill Crest Cemetery where there is a monument for him. If this is so, many wonder why he was not brought to Jackson to be buried by his wife as he wished. Perhaps it was impractical to bring the body this far in the summer heat. We may never know the answer.

Bradford's descendants are planning to erect a marker in Riverside for Darthula. Through the marking of her grave, Jackson will be closer to the fiery little general, a hero of the war with Mexico, even though he is not buried here.

10

MADISON COUNTY'S ROLE IN THE MEXICAN WAR

n 1846 the United States went to war with Mexico as a result of a boundary dispute fueled by American expansionist desire to control the entire North American continent. With an army of less than nine thousand men, the United States was ill prepared to fight a war on foreign soil. When the secretary of war requested twenty-eight hundred recruits from Tennessee, thirty thousand men responded. This is the origin of Tennessee being known as the Volunteer State. A lottery system was used to determine who would serve. Volunteers from West Tennessee comprised the Second Tennessee Infantry under the command of Colonel William T. Haskell

One hundred and eighteen men from Madison County answered the call. No training was done. There was no time for that. They just went to war. Some of these soldiers were still in their teens. One volunteer, George Wiley, looked so young that colonel Haskell refused to enlist him. Undaunted by this, Wiley hid under a wagon when the caravan left and was not discovered until they reached Brownsville. Haskell relented and accepted him, concluding that anyone who wanted to go that badly would make a good soldier.

General William T. Haskell.

Only a few days passed between the time the men signed up and their day of departure. On the evening of June 2, 1846, a large crowd assembled at the courthouse to witness the presentation of a flag made by the ladies of Jackson. Caroline Haskell, the colonel's daughter, presented the flag to Lieutenant Wiley Hale.

After dinner the company departed amid the waving of handkerchiefs and the tossing of hats, keeping step with Uncle King Anderson's drum and Aaron Day's fife. The first day they marched twenty miles, camping on the Hatchie River eight miles below Denmark. At Memphis they boarded steamboats to New Orleans and then proceeded by ship to Mexico.

The volunteers who went to fight in Mexico expected hardships and casualties from fighting. What they did not expect to encounter were the numbers who would fall to disease and the harsh Mexican climate. By October, 317 out of 588 members of the Second Tennessee were ill and had to be sent home or buried.

The Second Tennessee left camp at Camargo on December 8, 1946, and occupied Victoria on December 29. The regiment then became part of the army which was undertaking a campaign to march to Mexico City. A successful landing was made about two miles south of Vera Cruz, which was fortified and occupied by one thousand Mexican cavalry. The West Tennesseans finally got their first taste of battle when they were ordered to occupy a high sand hill some fifteen hundred feet above sea level. Skirmishing lasted for five minutes and then they were ordered to charge. Despite heavy fire, they succeeded in taking the hill without a single casualty. Lieutenant Wiley Hale of Jackson gave this account of the action.

The General then ordered the glorious 2nd Regt. (Col. Haskell's) to charge the heights and drive the force which was firing upon us. We gave a shout and commenced the charge amidst a shower

of bullets which fell around us like hail. You should have seen
our boys as they rushed up that hill with one continual shout of
defiance—though the hillside was covered with an almost
impenetrable "chaparral" (thicket of bushes) we gained the
summit of the height in less than 15 minutes. The Mexicans,
who has [sic] been firing upon us from this height, fled precipi-
tously upon our approach. We gave them a parting fire as they
ran down the hill towards the city which was in full view—
planted our flags—and gave three cheers for Tennessee and Col.
Haskell!

The first real fight for the Second Tennessee occurred in
the Battle of Cerro Gordo, a high hill which the Mexican
General Santa Anna held with thirteen thousand troops
opposing General Scott's Army of nine thousand soldiers. It
was in the action at Cerro Gordo that Colonel Haskell won
immortal honor for his bravery. An extra of the *Jackson
Republican* of May 7, 1847, told of the heavy losses on both
sides, the rough and rocky road through the dense Mexican
brush which was lined with American dead and wounded.
Seventeen pieces of artillery and the fire of two thousand
musketry played upon Colonel Haskell's force during the
engagement.

All the field officers of Colonel Haskell's command were
wounded except the colonel himself. Lieutenant Thomas
Ewell of the Rifles was very seriously wounded and later
died. Lieutenant Wiley Hale was seriously wounded and
also died. General Pillow had given the order for the
Second Tennessee to charge. A hurricane of grape, canister,
and musketry cut down one third of the men in three
minutes. Colonel Haskell assembled the scattered remnants
and reformed for a second charge. General Pillow coming
up asked, "Where is your command, Colonel? There are not
half of them here!" "There they are, Sir!" replied the
intrepid Haskell, pointing toward the enemy's batteries.
"There they are Sir, dead and dying on the field to which
they were ordered!"

Two of the heroes who made the supreme sacrifice, Lieutenant Hale and Lieutenant Ewell, were brought back to Jackson in sealed coffins and laid to rest at Riverside Cemetery. The Second Tennessee was mustered out at New Orleans on May 25, 1847. Colonel Haskell, eleven officers, and one hundred and seventy men, many of whom were sick and wounded of the Second Tennessee Regiment, arrived in Memphis on June 2, 1847. A hasty reception was held at the Gayoso Hotel before the colonel and his men from Madison County departed for the final lap of the journey homeward.

At a reception in Jackson, Haskell paid tribute to Lieutenant Ewell and displayed a few trophies of war, such as some "real live" Mexican boys and a brass six pounder which had been captured at Cerro Gordo.

The Mexican War was but a prelude to the Civil War fourteen years later. The loss of Southern soldiers at places like Shiloh made us forget about the volunteers who went to Mexico. The graves of Wiley Hale and Thomas Ewell at Riverside serve as silent reminders of their bravery long ago.

11

THE BATTLE OF BRITTON LANE

One hundred and thirty-nine years ago, on September 1, 1862, Madison County's most significant Civil War battle occurred near Denmark on an obscure country road called Britton Lane. The following is an account of that campaign.

It was late summer of the second year of the war, and throughout the South expectant eyes would soon watch two Confederate armies as they invaded Northern territory. One was under Robert E. Lee and was moving toward Maryland, and the other was under Braxton Bragg and was moving toward Kentucky. For the Confederacy, this was a time of hope. In April, the Confederacy had been on the defensive. New Orleans had been lost, McClellan was in front of Richmond, and Halleck was about to take Corinth. But by August the Southern nation was on the offensive.

In the west, Bragg's objective was to drive Buell out of Kentucky and Tennessee. In order to move against Buell, however, someone would have to keep U. S. Grant occupied in Western Tennessee and Northern Mississippi so that he could not send reinforcements to Buell. This job fell to Sterling Price, who was in command of the Army of the

West at Tupelo, Mississippi. To contain Grant and keep him from reinforcing Buell, Price planned to attack Rosecrans at Corinth, Mississippi, and to send cavalry raids to cut Grant's communications along the Mississippi Central Railroad in western Tennessee.

Before Price could use his cavalry, he had to reorganize them. The cavalry had been dismounted in Arkansas before Price assumed control and, as a result, his mounted forces numbered less than a thousand. To facilitate their reorganization, Frank C. Armstrong was promoted to brigadier general in charge of the cavalry. The new general had an unusual military background. He had served with the Union forces at the first Battle of Manassas, but afterwards had changed over to the Southern side. Prior to his taking over as head of the cavalry, he had been elected colonel of the Third Louisiana Infantry.

Armstrong's command left Guntown, Mississippi, at daybreak on Friday, August 22. For many of the raw troops, this was their first chance for action. Others in the various units had seen action at Shiloh and around Corinth, but, for all of them, it would be their first chance to act together as the cavalry of the Army of the West. When Armstrong left, he had four regiments plus one battalion of cavalry. These troops were Barteau's Second Tennessee Cavalry, the Second Arkansas Cavalry under Colonel W. F. Slemons, Wirt Adams's Cavalry, Wheeler's Cavalry, and Balch's Battalion. In all, they numbered about eleven hundred men. They were in good condition, and as one of the soldiers put it, "Generally speaking, they were a well mounted and fine looking bunch of men."

Armstrong moved his men along rapidly. Traveling southwest and then northwest, they covered forty-three miles in the first three days. The night of August 24 found them camped on the bank of Cypress Creek. On August 25, they marched sixteen miles to the Tippah River where they encamped, and on the following morning the leading regiment entered Holly Springs, Mississippi, as the town clock struck nine. After remaining in town for about ten minutes, they continued on to the north for five miles where they stopped and bivouacked on the banks of the Coldwater River.

While in the vicinity of Holly Springs, they were strengthened by three more cavalry regiments under the command of Colonel William H. Jackson. (Jackson, known as "Red" Jackson, was from Jackson, Tennessee. He was later promoted to general. He and Alexander Campbell were the two Confederate generals from Jackson, Tennessee.) These troops were the First Mississippi Cavalry under Colonel R. A. Pinson; the Second Missouri Cavalry under Colonel Robert McCulloch; and the Seventh Tennessee Cavalry under Colonel William H. Jackson. Jackson had been informed of the purpose of the raid, and previous to Armstrong's arrival had sent two spies to Jackson, Tennessee, to obtain information concerning the fortifications there. These two men—William Witherspoon of Jackson and Allen Shaw of Carroll County, Tennessee, both members of the Seventh Tennessee Cavalry—had been captured by a roving patrol of the Second Illinois Cavalry, but after having been taken to Jackson had managed to talk the Federal authorities into freeing them. Soon after this they made their way back to Holly Springs and joined their comrades.

The combined troops, now numbering around thirty-five hundred, rested in their camp until about 3:00 P.M. on the following afternoon. After breaking camp, they traveled close to sixteen miles, not stopping until late that night when they made their camp on a branch of the Wolf River within four miles of LaGrange, Tennessee. Here the horses and men rested. Armstrong realized that there would be little rest once contact had been made with the enemy.

In the saddle once again on Friday, August 29, the Confederates crossed the Memphis and Charleston Railroad at LaGrange, Tennessee. Leaving here around noon, they continued on to within nine miles of Bolivar where they spent the night. For some unexplained reason, the Federals in Bolivar were unaware of the danger that they were in, even though the rest of the surrounding outposts had been alerted. Later that same day, Colonel Marcellus M. Crocker, commander of the post, received a report that there was an enemy force of about four hundred men threatening him on the Guntown Road. Obviously, he was in for a big surprise.

The fight lasted throughout most of the day, progressing from a skirmish in the morning on the Van Buren Road to the bitterly contested fighting in the afternoon on the Middleburg Road. The Federals under Colonels Leggett and Force had done a creditable job in holding off superior forces all day without being captured. The Confederates under McCullough and Slemons had won a tactical victory in driving the Federals back into Bolivar, but it was an empty victory in that the Federals had escaped capture. Had the remainder of the Confederate cavalry been used, there would have been little chance for the Federals. There is little excuse for Armstrong's failure to employ all of his units.

The Federals reported their loss in the affair to be eighteen wounded, five killed, and sixty-four captured. The Federal estimate of the Confederate loss ran as high as two hundred, but this is only a guess as the Confederates did not indicate their losses. The only Confederate officer to be killed was Captain Champion of the Second Missouri Cavalry.

This was the first time that many of the Confederates had been under fire. Edwin H. Fay, a Louisiana soldier, remarked, "The Yanks fired on us with a battery of artillery and threw shell all around but did no damage, then ran back into Bolivar. We had five men wounded, two shot themselves after the battle, accidentally."

John Milton Hubbard of Company E Seventh Tennessee Cavalry observed, "Captain Champion of the Second Missouri was killed here. As his body was borne from the field of two of his troopers, I saw for the first time a dead Confederate who had been slain in battle."

The Confederates left the battlefield a little before sunset, going around to the west of Bolivar where they bivouacked for the night within three miles of Whiteville on Clearwater Creek. While the Confederates rested for a few hours, Yankee officials were hurriedly sending dispatches and rearranging forces. Armstrong had thrown a scare into top Union commanders, even though they were informed of his arrival. Now the Federals were faced with the problem of stopping Armstrong and his raiders before they could reach Jackson, Tennessee, which was described by Brigadier General Leonard R. Ross as being "weakly [sic] garrisoned and without fortifications."

To protect Jackson, the Federal force at Estanaula, Tennessee, under Colonel Dennis, was ordered to report to Jackson at once. This force consisted of the Twentieth Illinois Infantry under Captain Frisbie; the Thirtieth Illinois under Major Shedd; Gumbart's Artillery, which was Battery E of the Second Illinois Artillery; and two companies of cavalry under Captain John S. Foster, designated as the Fourth Ohio Cavalry companies. These troops struck tents on the morning of the thirty-first, destroying excess stores and baggage, and began their march toward Jackson.

Meanwhile, the Confederates encamped near Bolivar had eaten supper around 11:00 P.M. and had gone quickly to sleep. They were awakened about three hours later and began marching away from Bolivar before it was light. The command crossed the Big Hatchie River about daybreak and continued on until they struck the Mississippi Central Railroad at Toone, Tennessee. Here a detachment of Federal troops, stationed as railroad guards, began firing on the lead Confederates. The Confederates surrounded them and forced them to surrender before they could offer further resistance. Forty-two of the guards were captured and one was killed. A few Confederates were wounded.

About 3:00 P.M., as the column neared Medon, Federal pickets opened fire. The lead regiment, which was the Second Tennessee under Colonel C. R. Barteau, dismounted several of their members who carried long range rifles and opened fire. After a few shots, the Federal pickets retreated behind breastworks within the town.

The breastworks consisted of bales of cotton piled up near the railroad depot. Some of the detachments, which had been stationed in front of Medon, warned the Federals of the approaching danger. Consequently the breastworks of cotton had just been completed. Now about one hundred and fifty men of the Forty-fifth Illinois crouched behind them and awaited the arrival of the Confederates.

Barteau's Second Tennessee Infantry swung around to the right of the town and stormed the barricades from the northeast side. In the meantime, other regiments were coming into town and storming the breastworks from the front. The attackers were met with a steady fire from within the barricade, and the Confederates soon found that the Yankees could not be budged without the use of artillery; however, Armstrong had none at his disposal. The infantry continued firing on the barricades until about sundown when a train carrying six companies of the Seventh Missouri arrived. These troops disembarked and immediately charged, driving the Confederates before them. Darkness terminated further fighting, and the Federals soon retired within their breastworks around the depot. The Confederates drew off to the east where they settled down for the night on the Casey Savage farm just outside of Medon.

Losses for the engagement had been slight. The Yankees had had four killed and nine wounded. The Confederates had lost about twice that number. The attack had accomplished nothing. It would have been too bloody to have attacked the breastworks without artillery, and Armstrong wisely enough decided not to try it.

As the Confederates rested, other Federal troops were marching toward Medon to relieve the beleaguered garrison. These troops were the Federals who had been stationed at Estanaula under the command of Colonel Elias S. Dennis.

As has been previously stated, they had been ordered to report to Jackson to try to head off Armstrong. Colonel Lawler, commander of the post at Jackson, upon being informed of the attack on the garrison at Medon had quickly sent orders for these troops to turn around and march back to Medon. When the messenger reached Colonel Dennis and his command they were only about twelve miles out of Jackson. Dennis, however, turned his troops around and marched them back toward Medon. About ten that night, they reached Denmark where they encamped.

While the Federals rested at Denmark, the Confederates at the Casey Savage farm near Medon were going to bed without either fires or supper. Men in the Seventh Tennessee, who would later see service under Bedford Forrest, were beginning to make caustic remarks about the lack of food and provender. Years later, William Witherspoon of Company L Seventh Tennessee would recall, "My regiment, 7th Tennessee, was encamped near a corn-field, was without rations for man or beast . . . at a time, 1862, when the country was full of both . . . Our horses fared well and we did not grumble, like philosophers it was what would happen sometimes in a soldier's life."

Twenty-four hours later, scurrying away in retreat from the Federals at Britton Lane, the cavalry would have much harsher things to say about General Armstrong!

The Federal defenders at Medon received a pleasant surprise the next morning when the Confederates bypassed them. Passing to the west of the railroad and heading to the northwest, the Confederates were marching toward Denmark. At the same time, the Federals at Denmark were moving toward Medon, little suspecting that they were now marching right into the midst of Armstrong's column of cavalry. To shorten the distance, the Federals left the main road and began marching through a narrow road known as Britton Lane—an ordinary road fourteen feet in width with a deep gulley on either side between the fence and the road.

The Federal cavalry under Captain Foster was reconnoitering several miles in advance in the vicinity of the junction of the Denmark and Medon Roads, near the mouth of Britton Lane, when about ten that morning, Foster and his two companies of cavalry unexpectedly came upon the advance pickets of Armstrong's column. The Confederate pickets scurried off to inform Armstrong of the approaching troops, but for some unknown reason, it was almost noon when the pickets reached Armstrong with the news. Armstrong was eating lunch at a nearby house when he was informed that there were two regiments of infantry with supporting cavalry and artillery nearby.

Acting immediately, Armstrong led his troops forward a short distance and, upon reaching the vicinity of the mouth of Britton Lane, ordered his cavalry to dismount, throw every other lock of the fence, and then mount again. Armstrong's purpose in tearing down the fences was to facilitate a charge upon Dennis and his men as they marched down the lane.

In a moment the Confederates remounted, loaded their guns, and proceeded several hundred yards toward the lane, where they again came into contact with Foster's Cavalry. The lead Confederate regimen, the Second Missouri which had borne the brunt of the fighting at Bolivar, began firing away at the blue-clad horsemen and the action had begun!

The Federals, being greatly outnumbered, were forced to take a defensive position along a small ridge within a large grove of trees. They were further protected by a worn rail fence which stretched along the top of the ridge. The grove of trees was surrounded on all sides by cornfields, and Dennis selected a field in front of his infantry line to post his artillery. On the left of the artillery, within the trees, were posted companies B and G of the Twentieth Illinois. The remaining eight companies were posted on the right of the artillery.

Britton Lane Battlefield.

Once again, as they had been in every engagement throughout the entire raid, the Federals were badly outnumbered. With seven regiments and a battalion preparing to charge them, there is little doubt that the average Yankee in that line would have preferred to have been some place else! Outside of readying themselves and their guns, there was nothing that they could do but wait. One Yankee later wrote, "In front, and on the left and right were bare fields, swarming with rebels preparing for the charge. At last, on they came, the ground fairly trembling beneath their heavy tread. . . ."

The Illinois troops awaited the Confederates like veterans, and veterans they were, for they had already taken part in two large battles. In the operations around Fort Donelson the Twentieth Illinois had sustained losses of 132 men, including their lieutenant colonel, and a short time later the regiment lost 136 additional men at Shiloh. Following Shiloh, the men had seen little action until they were called upon to reinforce their comrades at Medon. The Union artillery opened fire on the Confederates and evidently surprised some of them. One of the members of a lead regiment wrote in a letter to his wife, "The Yanks were ambushed for us and the accursed Tories had led us right into it."

Armstrong, realizing that the artillery had the key to the battle, ordered McCulloch and Balch to take their men and charge the battery. Tearing down the intervening fences, the cavalry swarmed across the cornfield toward the battery. The Federals "loaded and fired as coolly as if they had been on a squirrel hunt," and the charging horsemen, finding the clouds of flying lead too much for them, were forced to retreat. On a second charge, the artillerymen momentarily abandoned their guns as the Confederate cavalry bore down upon them; but a strong fire from the Federal infantry prevented the cavalry from drawing the guns off. When the Confederate cavalry withdrew, the Federal gunners moved the artillery back closer to the woods so that a shallow ditch intervened between the cornfield and the guns.

Large dust clouds, raised by the charging cavalry, now partially obscured the field. Other Confederate regiments were now engaged in charging against the Federal infantry in the woods. Most of the Confederates dismounted and charged on foot, but concentrated rifle fire drove them back again and again. The Thirtieth Illinois, under Major Shedd, had come up by this time and had taken a position on the left of the Federal line.

Charging horsemen spurred their horses toward the Federal artillery a third and fourth time, but murderous rifle fire compelled them to withdraw again. On the fifth charge against the two guns, the Confederates were at last successful in capturing and drawing the cannon off. Just which regiment took the two guns was a matter that the veterans of the various regiments disputed years later when they came together at reunions and bivouacs. Almost all of the units took part in at least one of five charges against the artillery, so it does not really make any difference who captured them. The strongest claim is held by Company L of the Seventh Tennessee Cavalry, one of the last regiments to reach the battlefield. When the regiment came into contact with the Federals, General Armstrong ordered Company L to form fours and charge the artillery, while the remainder of the regiment was ordered to dismount and charge the infantry in the woods. The twenty members of Company L apparently caught the Federal artillerymen off guard and captured them before they could reverse positions and fire on the flying horsemen. William Witherspoon of that company later wrote, "As we got fairly started down the lane, we noticed they were ramming down the load. With a general impulse that the cannon had to be reached before it could be fired, we drove in our spurs and in a mad bound were upon them. It was then and there the old much-derided double barrel as an army gun done its work perfectly. In a second of time, we twenty, not one hurt, were all that were left alive with the two brass cannon."

The artillery was then taken to the east end of the lane where one piece of it was disabled and the other was thrown in a well. While this was going on, the other units were hurling themselves across the field right up to the fence where the Yankees were posted. The result of this was appalling, as evidenced by the gray-clad figures that littered the field. Some of the Confederates succeeded in reaching the fence only to be killed upon trying to climb over it. Company E Seventh Tennessee Cavalry came under such a heavy fire near the fence, that one member of that company, John Milton Hubbard, later wrote, "How so many men ever got out of that field alive is one of those unaccountable things that sometimes occur in war."

About 3:00 P.M., Armstrong decided that he had had enough and called off the remaining Confederates. Dusk on that September afternoon found them moving slowly toward the Hatchie River. (At the time they had eighty Federal prisoners with them which slowed them considerably.) Not stopping at dark, they continued on until about 3:00 A.M. when they stopped near the Hatchie River. Behind them they left one hundred and seventy nine dead whom the Federals buried in common graves. Many more wounded comrades had been left in houses surrounding the battlefield to await treatment of their wounds.

Most of the Confederates were discouraged by the outcome of the battle, feeling that Armstrong had handled his forces poorly. On previous nights they had complained because of lack of food for themselves and for their horses. Now they were beginning to question Armstrong's ability as a commander. Years later Confederate reminiscences would contain such references as this, "We were certainly on the run, to say the least, a forced march, not halting or stopping until we ferried across the Hatchie, six miles distant, on a ferry boat. Where does the blame lie? Certainly not with the men, they carried out every order and executed it as completely as the 7th Tennessee did."

Another wrote, "The whole command was discouraged by the operations of this raid, and thought that, if we had gained anything at all, we had paid dearly for it."

Obviously the Confederates had good reason to be unhappy. Simply by encircling the Yankee regiments, Armstrong could probably have secured their capture. Instead he chose to send regiment after regiment across an open field to certain destruction.

One Confederate later compared Armstrong with the "Wizard of the Saddle," Nathan Bedford Forrest, and decided, "Is it not shameful that our troops were so managed as to suffer a loss of such magnitude with no corresponding good? What if Forrest had been there instead of Armstrong? Colonel Dennis would have been crushed as easily as an eggshell, with not probably the loss of one-half a dozen men." Instead, the Federals, being well protected by the woods and fences, received a trifling loss of four killed and about sixty-five wounded.

On September 2, the Confederate command crossed the Big Hatchie River about ten miles below where they had crossed before. By midnight on September 3, the dusty column had retraced its way back to within five miles of LaGrange, Tennessee. After this, there were no more actions with the Federals. All that was left for them to do was to return to their Mississippi base on the Mobile and Ohio Railroad. By September 7 they were in Ripley, Mississippi, after having rested for two days on the Wolf River. From Ripley they traveled on a direct northern route back to their base. By the eighth, they were within twelve miles of Baldwin, Mississippi. On September 9, the weary Confederates came into Baldwin and the raid was at an end.

Tactically speaking, they had accomplished their mission in that they had diverted Grant from sending further reinforcements to Don Carlos Buell. Militarily speaking, however, Armstrong had allowed himself to be outmaneuvered by much smaller forces. In all of the actions that he had commanded, he had evidenced a basic lack of knowledge of tactics. But brighter days were ahead for Armstrong. In later years of the war, he would become a trusted leader under Bedford Forrest.

For the cavalry of the Army of the West, there was little chance to rest. On the day after they returned to Baldwin, they were called upon to take part in the campaign of Sterling Price, which resulted in the Battle of Iuka, Mississippi. In this campaign the cavalry performed in an efficient manner and it became obvious that their campaign into Western Tennessee had given them experience if nothing else.

Today, almost a hundred and thirty-nine years since General Armstrong and his butternut cavalry came sweeping down through West Tennessee, there are few traces left of the raid. At the Battle of Britton Lane, near Denmark, Tennessee, there are two monuments. One of these is an obscure stone marker which stands about fifty feet away from the roadside. The inscription on this marker reads, "Erected by John Ingram Bivouac, September 1, 1897, to honor an unknown number of Confederate soldiers who fell in battle on this field, September 1, 1862, and many of whom are buried here."

The second monument is not a stone marker but a home that has existed since long before the battle. It was about a mile away from the battlefield and was used as a hospital after the battle. The long front has two rooms with a dog-trot between them. An "L" in the rear, also with a wide gallery, serves as a dining room and kitchen. At the time of the battle, a small room stood at the far right end of the gallery. Here, after the battle, the bodies of many dead and wounded soldiers were stretched out. Bloodstains could be seen on this floor for a number of years. The room was eventually destroyed and made into a part of the front gallery, however, and rain and time have erased the stains of the soldiers who lay there.

The occupant of the house is also an historical figure. He is Jim Lewis "Big Hat" Collins who has lived in the house for fifty-eight years now. In 1897, just before the monument was dedicated, Collins and other neighborhood residents searched the battlefield and gathered up all of the relics they could find. Their relics included buttons, gun parts, brass rings, and bits of bone. The graves of the Confederate soldiers were also excavated and the remains found in these graves, along with the other relics, were buried just behind and to the right of the stone monument on the battlefield. Today there is a small mound which marks the site of these relics.

For years, members of the John Ingram Bivouac would gather on the old battlefield to tell their stories of the battle. Although those soldiers are long since dead, the monument stands, almost forgotten, as a symbol of the bravery of the men who died there so long ago.

THE MAGIC BUTTONS

The old Presbyterian Cemetery at Denmark sits high on a hill on the left side of the road, just before you come to the little town. It is lonesome up on that hill with large ancient cedars overlooking the graves. In the southwest corner of the cemetery three confederate soldiers are buried. There used to be four.

Some three miles south of Denmark the Battle of Britton Lane was fought on September 1, 1862. It is the largest Civil War battle site in Madison County. There a Confederate cavalry raiding party fought two regiments of Illinois infantry with supporting artillery and cavalry. Four times that day the Confederate charged the Federal line with disastrous results, leaving 186 fallen comrades dead. Federal casualties, due to the nature of the terrain, were slight. Following the battle the Confederate commander, Brigadier General Frank C. Armstrong, retreated with his troops to Estanaula Landing where they crossed the Hatchie River and retired to North Mississippi.

On the day after the battle the fallen Confederates were buried in a long slit trench. Those bodies were to remain there until 1898, when they were dug up and reburied on

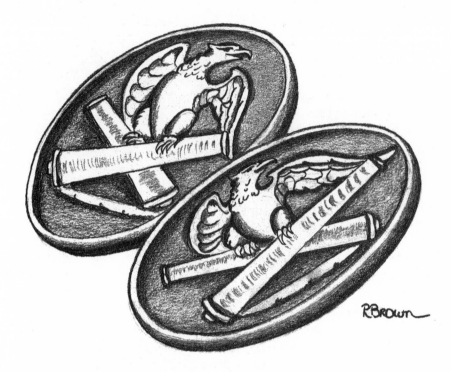

Buttons from Revolutionary War.

the thirty-sixth anniversary of the battle at a newly dedicated stone monument. They remain there today.

Among the dead was the body of a young soldier still in his teens. Because of his age, the burial party hesitated to bury him in the mass grave. Ultimately it was decided to bury him in the Presbyterian Cemetery along with Dr. Joe Allen of Whiteville and Ed Peters. C. W. Henry picked the site for the graves. Before placing the bodies in the ground he noticed some odd looking buttons on the coat of the young soldier. Henry cut two of the buttons from the coat and later gave them to Captain Guthrie who identified them as buttons from the Revolutionary War. Strangely enough Guthrie kept the buttons and carried them in his pocket as a momento of the young soldier. Years later, when attending a Confederate reunion in Atlanta, he met an old woman named Jefferson. While exchanging war reminiscences, she told him of her young son who slept in an unmarked grave in some faraway battlefield. She had refused to let him join the army because of his age, but he had run away to join the fight. She never heard from him except once when he had written to request clothes to be sent to him at Bolivar, Tennessee. She had made him a uniform coat from an old dress. To give it a military touch she had attached buttons from her grandfather's coat. He had been a soldier under "Mad Anthony Wayne" in the Revolutionary War at the Battle of Stoney Point. She sent the uniform but never heard from him. Without saying a word, Guthrie produced the buttons. You can imagine the effect it had when Mrs. Jefferson recognized those buttons, placed on a boy's coat so long ago.

The story had a happy ending. Mrs. Jefferson journeyed to Denmark from Atlanta to claim her son's body. The problem was that C. W. Henry, who dug the grave, was long dead. Finally an old Negro man, Shedrick Pipkins, remembered where the grave was located. Mrs. Jefferson had the body taken back to Atlanta where he was buried in the family cemetery. But what a strange story. Was it just a coincidence that Captain Guthrie, who was around thousands of soldiers who were killed in battle, would keep the buttons for almost twenty-five years and would end up showing them to Mrs. Jefferson. As the old saying goes, truth is often stranger than fiction!

13

FORREST'S WEST TENNESSEE RAID OF 1862

Jackson and its surrounding counties have few Civil War battlefields. Most people prefer to tour the Battle of Shiloh, about an hour away on the Tennessee River near Savannah. Jackson and Madison County suffered under Federal occupation for exactly one year from April 1862 to April 1863, but little fighting occurred. Our major battleground is Britton Lane near Denmark. Most of our battle sites center around Nathan Bedford Forrest's two raids into West Tennessee. The first of these occurred from December 10, 1862, to January 3, 1863. This is the story of that campaign.

As 1862 drew to a close, Nathan Bedford Forrest's star as a military commander was beginning to rise. He had performed brilliantly at the Battle of Fort Donelson when he broke with the other defeated Confederate generals and refused to surrender. Riding out in a blinding snowstorm, he led his troops to safety. A few months later, at the Battle of Shiloh, he discovered that Don Carlos Buell with his Army of the Ohio was reinforcing Grant's troops on the night of April 6. His attempts to convince Confederate commanders to resume the attack failed. The next day,

Beauregard's Confederate Army was soundly defeated as Forrest had predicted.

Forrest had no formal military training. Nor had he graduated from West Point, as did many of his contemporaries. In 1862 he was viewed as a partisan raider and was treated accordingly by Jefferson Davis. Throughout the early fall of 1862, he operated his command in Middle Tennessee. While Forrest was in Middle Tennessee, U. S. Grant struggled with logistical problems in West Tennessee. His objective was to supply a Northern Army advancing from West Tennessee through Northern Mississippi with Vicksburg as its destination. Grant's supplies were drawn entirely by rail from a base at Columbus, Kentucky, with a line of supply along the Mobile and Ohio Railroad through Jackson, Tennessee, to Corinth, Mississippi, and another from Jackson along the Mississippi Central Railroad through Bolivar and Grand Junction. Grant's headquarters were at Holly Springs, Mississippi.

Lieutenant General John C. Pemberton, just put in command of the inadequate Confederate forces in Mississippi, appealed for help. General Braxton Bragg, Forrest's commander, responded that he would send a cavalry raid into West Tennessee to disrupt Grant's supply lines. The hope was that Grant would have to retreat back into West Tennessee, relieving the pressure on Vicksburg.

Such a plan was nearly impossible. Forrest protested that more than half of his twenty-one hundred men were armed with ancient flintlock rifles, some dating back to the War of 1812. Flints and ammunition were dangerously limited. Some soldiers were unarmed. Winter in West Tennessee was now upon them. The roads had turned to bottomless mud, making it near impossible to pull their artillery. They would be in enemy territory at all times, exposed to constant attack. Protests and objections were overruled. Obeying orders, Forrest, then forty-five miles south of Nashville, started out on December 10, 1862. His first dilemma was how to get into West Tennessee. By then the Tennessee River was swollen and icy. He determined to cross the river at Clifton, some seventy-five miles away. Arriving there on December 15, he had two small flatboats constructed. It took two nights and a day in freezing rain to cross the river. Luckily no Yankee gunboats appeared. Marching eight miles west of the river, they built their first fires in two days. Though they were safely across the river, the Federal commander at Jackson, Brigadier General Jere C. Sullivan, had received a telegraph that Forrest had crossed the river at Clifton and was moving toward him. The wheels were beginning to turn. With this timely notice, Grant ordered a concentration of men at Jackson to protect the railroads, ordering men there by rail from Oxford, Corinth, and Bolivar as well as men from the garrisons at Forts Heiman, Henry, and Donelson.

The first encounter with Federal troops occurred at Beech Creek, five miles east of Lexington, when they were met by a cavalry column under the command of Colonel Robert G. Ingersoll, consisting of an Illinois regiment, the Second West Tennessee Cavalry, a battalion from Ohio, and an Indiana artillery battery of two guns. Skirmishing as they went, the Federal troops fell back five miles to the outskirts of Lexington, forming a battle line where the artillery covered two roads at the crossing of a creek.

While Forrest demonstrated in their front, troops of the Fourth Alabama swept to the north around the Yankee's left flank. Ingersoll's commanders reported that the enemy was pouring in from all directions. A precipitous retreat followed and the fight was soon over. One of Forrest's troopers wrote afterwards ". . . but if he really believed there is no hell, we convinced him that there was something mightily like it." One hundred and fifty Yankees were captured along with Colonel Ingersoll and the two Indiana cannons. Upon being captured, Ingersoll's first remark was, "Hell, what a mess!" Asked if the prisoners were all his men, he replied "these are the Illinoisans, the Tennesseeans have ingloriously fled."

Ingersoll and his men remained prisoners for three days until they were paroled and released. During this time, Ingersoll played poker with his Confederate captors, losing all of his money. The captured artillery pieces would serve Forrest throughout the war.

The remnants of Ingersoll's command fell back twenty miles to within four miles of Jackson. Ingersoll believed that Forrest had five thousand men with eight pieces of artillery. Other rumors circulated that he had at least ten thousand men.

The Confederate victory at Lexington sent a wave of panic through Federal occupied West Tennessee though Forrest had only twenty-one hundred men, half of whom were unarmed or had obsolete weapons. Federal estimates of his force were much higher. Some Federal commanders estimated that he had as many as ten thousand mounted troops. Forrest, up to his usual tricks, marched his troops back and forth with kettledrums beating at widely separated positions to give the impression of marching infantry. One woman asked Private Tom Jones of the Fourth Tennessee how many soldiers they had. He replied, "Madam, I would tell you if I could. Do you know how many trees there are standing in West Tennessee? Well, we've got enough men to put one behind each tree, and two or three behind the biggest ones."

Brigadier General Jere Sullivan, the Union Commander at Jackson, felt that he was greatly outnumbered, though he had four times the number of troops to oppose Forrest. Accordingly he began gathering more troops to meet the threat. A brigade of Iowa soldiers stationed at Corinth, en route home for Christmas furlough, was ordered off the train in Jackson. They were then ordered to defend the train depot "to the last extremity and if overpowered . . . to retire to the Courthouse." On the same evening, more troops were brought to Jackson from Bolivar.

Colonel Adolph Englemann was ordered to advance east from Jackson on the Lexington Road toward Cotton Grove Road with the Forty-third and Sixty-first Illinois infantry regiments. He was also ordered to take command of any troops he encountered retreating from Lexington. About three and one-half miles out of town he was joined by the Fifth Ohio Cavalry, the Eleventh Illinois Cavalry, and the Second West Tennessee Cavalry, all retreating from Lexington.

Colonel Englemann pulled his troops back and placed the cavalry in front as a skirmish line and sent patrols out on his flanks. The infantry camped in a field not far from Salem Cemetery. The day had been unusually warm, and many of the Federal soldiers left their coats at the depot. The night turned very cold, especially since fires were forbidden which could give away their position. Confederate camp fires to the east made it seem even colder. Corporal Leander Stillwell of the Sixty-first Illinois described the night as bitter cold. The men would pile on top of each other to stay warm. Soon the men on the bottom would become uncomfortable and the pile would shift again with others going to the bottom.

In the early morning hours of December 19, the Sixty-first Illinois was posted in line behind Salem Cemetery and the Forty-third Illinois was posted on the south side of the road. The Union Cavalry was posted in front of the infantry. Just after sunrise Forrest sent two Cavalry companies under Colonel T. G. Woodward and Colonel J. B. Biffle's Cavalry battalion west toward them. After skirmishing for a few moments, the Union Cavalry fell back to the main battle line where the infantry was concealed. When the Confederate Column reached thirty to fifty yards of the cemetery, the Union infantry opened fire. The Confederates, unaware of the Union infantry before the shots rang out, fell back in confusion with several casualties. One Confederate, at the head of the column, was riding a white horse and drew much of the fire. After the battle, the only clue was a discarded sock covered in blood! Six of the Confederate horses, without riders, continued on through the line creating great confusion. The Union commander, Colonel Englemann, lost

Battle of Salem Cemetery.

control of his horse, Bragg, who broke and ran away following the confederate horses for some distance before Englemann got the horse under control and returned.

Forrest then brought up Captain Freeman's artillery battery, which began shelling the Union line. As a bit of irony, one of the cannons Freeman was using was a Yankee gun captured the day before in Lexington. Colonel Englemann reported, "Fortunately only a few of the shells exploded—some went over our heads into the woods and hit trees and exploded, but we suffered no loss."

The Union Cavalry, displaying the same timidity as the day before, began to fall back, exposing the flanks and creating confusion as they retreated through the infantry. The Federals held their position for another thirty minutes, despite being shelled by the confederate cannons and fearful of being attacked on their flanks. During this time Colonel Dengler of the Sixty-first Illinois went in front of their position and brought in three Confederates who had the misfortune of having their horses shot out from under them. As the Confederate shells began landing closer, one man was killed and three were wounded. At this point Colonel Englemann began withdrawing his troops, and for all practical purposes the fight was over. When Federal reinforcements arrived, they advanced again only to find that Forrest was gone, leaving only the cold ashes of his camp fires where he had been.

14

PRIVATE JAMES COBLE, CSA, LOST AND FOUND

Following his appearance near Jackson, Forrest's real objective began to transpire. To defeat the ten thousand troops at Jackson was never his plan. Simply put, he only wanted the Federals to believe he would attack Jackson, while his plan was to destroy the Mobile and Ohio Railroad north and south of Jackson.

On the same day of the fight at Salem Cemetery, Forrest's Tenth Tennessee Cavalry headed south with an objective of burning the bridge over the south fork of the Forked Deer River on the M and O Railroad. A blockhouse was constructed on the site manned by Company C of the 106th Illinois Infantry. The Illinois infantry was under the command of Captain D. H. Hart of Lincoln, Illinois.

Members of the Tenth Tennessee reached the site just as an early December dusk settled over the blockhouse. Lights could be seen inside the little fort through the gun ports. As the Confederates crept closer, suddenly all of the lights inside the blockhouse were extinguished. The raiders realized that the Yankees were about to open fire. Just as rifle fire broke out inside the fort, one of the Confederates named Dave Mathis jumped off the tracks and yelled, "get off quick." Some were slow to react and one of the Confederates was killed. In the dark, they could only guess at the identity of the fallen soldier. Another Confederate, John Bates, ran his hands over the body to see who it was. He realized that his fallen comrade was Private James Coble. He was able to identify him by a mole skin cap that Coble wore. In addition, there was only one man killed and Coble was missing the next morning.

Realizing that the element of surprise was gone, the Confederates withdrew, aborting the mission. On the morning after the battle, Hart's soldiers found Coble's body

James Coble marker.

on the edge of the tracks. Hart described him as a young man with red hair in an unusually clean uniform. He was buried near the spot where he fell. An elderly lady named Harris, who lived near the site, reported that Federal soldiers dug up the body seven days later, believing that the fallen soldier was a Yankee. When they realized that he was a Confederate soldier, the body was covered up again.

This is the story of one soldier who was killed. Why then, with so many other casualties, would it be remarkable? Private Coble's family never knew what happened to him. His wife died, years later, wondering if and where he died.

Now comes the remarkable part of the story. Apparently Captain Hart never forgot about the young Confederate who was killed just outside of the blockhouse. In 1914, fifty-two years later, Hart wrote an open letter to the *Jackson Sun* and the *Commercial Appeal* describing the gravesite. He also wrote to the Jackson chief of police. James Coble Jr., then the mayor of Union City, read the letter and realized that this was probably his father. After corresponding with members of his family and Confederate veterans, it became apparent that the fallen soldier was indeed his father. After visiting the site, he purchased a marble monument for three hundred dollars to mark the grave. In a war that nearly destroyed the country, the spirit of healing is apparent in Captain Hart's efforts, more than half a century after the war's end.

Today the marker stands just south of Harts Bridge Road near the railroad. It is a fitting memorial to a brave young soldier and a Yankee captain who never forgot him. (Private James Coble is the great-grandfather of Doctor Charles Cox of Jackson, a noted collector of Confederate side arms.)

While Forrest's main force made a mock attack on Yankee troops just east of Jackson, portions of his command headed north and south of Jackson with the intent of tearing up the M and O Railroad to disrupt General Sherman's supply routes. While the Tenth Tennessee Cavalry was unable to destroy the railroad bridge over the Forked Deer River (just south of Jackson near the Harts Bridge Road), Colonel George G. Dibrell's command had better luck. Striking first eight miles north of Jackson at Carroll Station they captured 102 soldiers of the 106th Illinois. (Ironically another company from this regiment had repulsed the Confederate attack on the Hart's Bridge Road.) Gaining much needed guns and ammunition, they tore up the railroad tracks and switches.

Continuing on toward Humboldt they attempted to destroy the bridge over the Forked Deer River between Jackson and Humboldt. Just as they attacked the stockade garrison, it was defended by a trainload of reinforcements from Jackson. While they fired on the garrison, with little effect, a portion of their command moved on to Humboldt. Attacking at a spot where the Memphis and Ohio Railroad crossed the Mobile and Ohio Railroad they had immediate success. Here they destroyed portions of the track, trestles, and rolling stock. When the depot and surrounding buildings were set on fire, there was an accompanying display of fireworks from ammunition stored in the buildings. More than one hundred Federals were captured.

Little did the Federal commanders realize what Forrest was up to. First sending six regiments of Yankee infantry east of Jackson to find Forrest, they were soon followed by all but two thousand troops who remained to guard Jackson. Forrest found nothing but old campfires. As the fires burned at Humboldt, Forrest continued on to Trenton where the largest garrison between Jackson and Columbus was located. The stockade was made of bales of cotton and hogsheads of tobacco. In addition, Federal sharpshooters were in two brick buildings adjacent to the stockade. Arriving about three o'clock on December 20, Forrest personally led the charge. Federal fire killed two of his men and wounded seven. Changing tactics, the Confederates then encircled the garrison and opened fire with artillery. At the third firing, a white flag was run up and the entire garrison surrendered. Two hundred Federals had been captured at Humboldt and another seven hundred at Trenton along with two colonels and nine other officers. In addition to the prisoners, Forrest captured twenty thousand rounds of artillery, four hundred thousand rounds of small arms ammunition, and one hundred thousand rations. One item in the capture was a large amount of counterfeit Confederate money. The engraving was so much better than real Confederate notes that it was unusable. The men used it for playing poker! Forrest claimed a saber of the United States dragon pattern for himself. After he had its regulation dull edge sharpened to a razor sharp edge, he used it for the rest of the war.

While the Confederates were refitting, Forrest paroled the twleve hundred prisoners already taken. Up to his old tricks, he made sure the prisoners would carry back an exaggerated estimate of his command. He did this by having courier after courier come up with imaginary orders for nonexistent generals to move up with their commands. As night settled over Trenton, campfires were built here and there. After dark, detachments were marched back and forth, giving the impression of fresh reinforcements coming to join Forrest. On Sunday morning the prisoners were marched north under a flag of truce to Columbus where they were expected to be shipped home.

After burning everything he could not carry, Forrest moved north on December 21, toward Union City. At Rutherford two companies of Federals were captured and the railroad trestles, bridges, and tracks were destroyed from Trenton to Kenton. At Kenton he captured Colonel Thomas J. Kinney of the 119th Illinois and 250 of his men.

The destruction of a large railroad trestle and the crossing of the Obion River kept them busy until the afternoon of the twenty-second, when they moved north toward Union City. At 4:00 P.M. on December 23, they charged into that town and captured 106 Federal troops without firing a gun! The Federal commander, Captain Samuel B. Logan, reported that within three minutes of seeing the Confederates they were completely surrounded.

Forrest had now reached the Kentucky border, which he crossed later that same day. On Christmas Eve his troops were busy destroying railroad trestles near Moscow, Kentucky, and other bridges over the north and south forks of the Obion River. By Christmas Day he had completed his mission of destroying the Mobile and Ohio Railroad from Jackson to Moscow, Kentucky. They had destroyed every bridge except the one south of Humboldt. Not a yard of trestlework was left standing, not a foot of culvert was left undestroyed, and the rails over much of the distance had been ruined for future use by building fires on the tracks which caused the rails to expand and buckle. Nervous Federal commanders reported that Cairo, Columbus, and Paducah were in danger of being captured.

With his mission at an end, Forrest then concentrated his efforts on how to escape out of West Tennessee. Forrest's raid into West Tennessee had been successful far beyond expectation. But now Federal troops were closing in from all directions. On Christmas Day, 1862, Forrest left Union City starting southwest along the Northwestern Railroad toward the Tennessee River. At the same time General Sullivan left Jackson in pursuit of him.

On the day after Christmas, drenching rains began turning roads into bottomless mud. By the morning of the twenty-eighth, when Forrest turned south from McKenzie's Station, the south fork of the Obion River was at flood stage with only one abandoned bridge remaining. In a wire to General U. S. Grant, General Sullivan reported, "I have Forrest in a tight place . . . The gunboats are up the river as far as Clifton and have destroyed all bridges and ferries. . . . My troops are moving on him from three directions, and I hope with success."

Forrest's only hope was to repair the decaying bridge across the Obion. In doing so, it took them all night to get across. Forrest guided the first wagon team across, but the next two teams slipped in. Having no sandbags, deep muddy holes were filled in with captured bags of coffee and sugar! Emerging from the Obion bottoms, he faced the prospects of fighting four separate groups of Federal soldiers, each as large as his own. General Sullivan had two brigades between Forrest and the Tennessee River. A mixed force under Colonel Lowe was coming toward him from Fort Henry near Paris. Coming up from Corinth, where Forrest hoped to cross to safety, was General Granville Dodge whose troops were closer to Clifton than Forrest. Yet another brigade was moving out of Jackson under Colonel Lawler.

Forrest had about two thousand men in his command. They had been on the move for several days without sleep or rest. Hiding in the edge of the Obion bottoms, Forrest's scouts watched a brigade of Federal infantry pass by under the command of Colonel Cyrus Dunham. Coming from the direction of Trenton, Dunham arrived at Huntingdon on December 29. Following just behind, Forrest slipped his command into McLemoresville. A few miles to the west, Colonel John Fuller and three Ohio regiments were moving toward Huntingdon along with Federal General Jeremiah C. Sullivan.

Forrest was now forced to choose between fleeing toward the Tennessee River or staying and fighting. Finding himself between two Federal armies, he determined to attack and destroy Dunham's brigade and then turn on Colonel Fuller. Early on the morning of December 31, Dunham moved his brigade to Parker's Cross Roads expecting to be joined there by Fuller's brigade.

Forrest sent four companies of cavalry to watch for and skirmish with Fuller, preventing them from coming in behind Forrest's battle line at the crossroads. Forrest intended to fight the first battle primarily with artillery saving his cavalry to fight Fuller's brigade later in the day. The plan seemed to go according to plan. The Federals were driven back beyond the crossroads by mid-morning, retiring into heavy woods. From this position they made several desperate charges on the Confederate artillery but were driven back. The Federal artillery, consisting of three guns, was captured during this period. Unable to hold their lines, the Federals retreated again to a third position, retiring in confusion to a stand of trees of about sixty acres enclosed by a fence and surrounded by open fields. By this time, elements of Forrest's command had gained the rear of the position capturing the entire wagon and ammunition train. Surrounded on all sides, white flags of surrender began to be waved up and down the Federal line. Just as total victory was in his grasp, the unexpected happened. As the conditions of surrender were about to be discussed the sounds of rifle fire were heard. With Forrest's scouts watching the wrong road, General Sullivan's troops had come in behind him and were now moving to attack. Never before, or since, had Forrest been so surprised. In his report he stated, "I could not believe that they were Federals until I rode up myself into their lines." When asked by an aide what to do, Forrest was quoted as saying, "Charge both ways."

Even though he was between two separate Federal commands, Forrest was able to extricate his troops and escape toward Lexington. About three hundred of his dismounted troops were captured. Amazingly, General Sullivan made no move to pursue the Confederates. By January 1, Forrest reached the Tennessee River and crossed to safety.

The campaign had lasted for fifteen days from December 17 to January 1. For one week of this period there was heavy rain, sleet, and snow. In a country notorious for bad roads he had marched with artillery and wagons more than three hundred miles. Of the Union troops he opposed, he had killed, wounded, or captured more than fifteen hundred men, captured five pieces of artillery, eleven caissons, and thirty-eight wagon teams. All of his men had new guns, ammunition, blankets, and equipment. His destruction of Grant's supply lines would delay the attack on Vicksburg by six months. Forrest's losses were less than five hundred.

The success of the expedition resulted in a vote of thanks from the Confederate Congress in Richmond. Forrest's commander, General Braxton Bragg, made the following report:

General Forrest proceeded with his brigade of cavalry to West Tennessee. His command was composed chiefly of new men, imperfectly armed and equipped, and in his route lay the Tennessee River, which had to be crossed by such means as could be hastily improvised. The result of his expedition has been most brilliant and decisive. The enemy, in consequence of this vigorous assault in a quarter vital to their self-preservation, have been compelled to throw back a large force from the Mississippi, and virtually abandon a campaign which so seriously threatened our safety. The loss of Forrest, though considerable, is small in comparison with the results achieved and the loss of the enemy. He has received my thanks, and deserves the applause of his government.

15

NATHAN BEDFORD FORREST AT ESTANAULA LANDING

onsidering the circumstances, it appeared that Christmas of 1863 would be a sad affair. Even though Jackson's year-long occupation by Federal soldiers had ended on June 6, the war seemed to last forever. Gettysburg had been fought and Vicksburg lost. The entire Mississippi River was controlled by Yankee troops and gunboats. Food was scarce and morale was low as news trickled home of loved ones killed or wounded on far away battlefields. And then Nathan Bedford Forrest came calling.

For the second time in two years, Forrest came back to West Tennessee to gather much needed recruits and supplies. In October of that year he had been assigned to a new command in West Tennessee. He had only 279 men! At the time, Forrest was a brigadier general. On December 4, he was promoted to major general.

In mid-November Forrest arrived at Okolona, Mississippi, and established headquarters there. His first assignment was to proceed into West Tennessee, behind enemy lines, to gather an army. He would be surrounded by Federal soldiers of the Sixteenth Corps with garrisons at Memphis, Columbus, Fort Pillow near Ripley, Fort Heiman

Nathan Bedford Forrest.

near Paris, and another at Paducah. With such a small force available to him, General Sherman had contemptuously wired to General Hurlburt at Memphis stating, "Forrest may cavort about the country as much as he pleases." Sherman would soon regret this statement.

At Okolona he was joined by two other commands numbering about four hundred men. Many of these soldiers had neither guns nor horses. Immediately he began organizing to break through the Federal lines along the Memphis and Charleston Railroad, march into West Tennessee, and establish his headquarters at Jackson. Faced with a shortage of horses he was forced to leave a third of his command behind. In addition, he had to leave two of his four cannons. On December 1, he headed north with five light wagons loaded with ammunition. Faking attacks on Memphis, he crossed safely into West Tennessee near Saulsbury. No Federal troops were encountered until they reached the Hatchie River at Bolivar, which was guarded by the Sixth Illinois commanded by Colonel Edward Hatch. The Federal troops were driven away when Colonel Hatch was shot through the lung. By December 6, Forrest was at Jackson.

Forrest's chief of artillery, Captain John W. Morton, described the reaction of the citizens in Bolivar and Jackson: "General Forrest found everywhere an eager welcome . . . At Bolivar there was a big wedding, one of General Forrest's men marrying a belle of the town. At Jackson, abundant food, forage and entertainment were provided by the patriotic ladies. Dinners, parties and other gayeties were treats to the weary soldier after the long marching and insufficient supplies."

By December 7, Forrest was busy setting up recruiting camps, usually in remote sections of the county. Each day fifty to one hundred men signed up, including one hundred Kentuckians who switched over from the Federals. By December 13, he was able to send his first new regiment south. At the same time horses, cattle, wagons, and forage were being gathered. (Forrest spent twenty thousand dollars of his own money in this endeavor, hoping to be paid back by the Confederacy.)

As Christmas grew closer it bacame apparent that he could not remain in Jackson much longer. On December 18, five separate Federal commands began closing in on Jackson—altogether fifteen thousand men went after Forrest's command which numbered about thirty-five hundred men, one thousand of which were unarmed.

On the night of December 22, a dance was given at the courthouse in Jackson at which all the city was present. The dancing was kept up all night and the soldiers headed south at dawn on the twenty-third. To escape, Forrest would have to cross the Hatchie and the Wolf Rivers, both at flood stage. Once across the rivers, it would be necessary to cross the railroad again, with troop trains ready to run either way to interrupt him. To add to his difficulties, he was encumbered with a wagon train along with two hundred cattle and three hundred hogs.

While the main body moved south toward Estanaula Landing on the Hatchie River, another column under the command of Colonel D. M. Wisdom headed southeast to meet and fend off a Federal Column from Corinth. Striking the Federal Column near Jack's Creek, a noisy fight ensued with the Federals eventually retreating south toward Corinth. After an all night march of thirty miles, Wisdom's men rejoined the main command on Christmas morning. Forrest and his escort were the last to leave Jackson, heading south toward Estanaula Landing about six o'clock on Christmas Eve. Prior to this, Colonel Tyree Bell had departed with the main body of soldiers, some twenty-five hundred men, many of whom were unarmed. Colonel R. V. Richardson was sent ahead with an advance detachment to secure the crossing at Estanaula Landing and to seize the last remaining ferryboat on the river. General Sherman wired ahead that a heavy cavalry force should be sent against Forrest to "get on his heels and chase him to the wall." General Hurlbut added, "I think we shall cure Forrest of his ambition to command West Tennessee."

Forrest and his escort arrived at Estanaula Landing about 10:00 P.M. on Christmas Eve, where he found his main force struggling to cross the swollen freezing Hatchie with its wide flooded bottoms. Five miles away, on the south side of the river, a Federal force of six hundred men were bivouacked blocking the escape route. Pushing on across the river, Forrest and his escort of sixty men charged straight into the Federal camp. The attack was not made in an ordinary formation but in a single line of troopers spread ten paces or so apart, so that the sixty men of the company formed a line more than a quarter of a mile long. With his line so formed and with every junior officer and sergeant instructed to pick up and repeat orders as if he was commanding at least a company in a brigade drill, Lieutenant Nathan Boone, commanding the escort, roared out the order, "Brigade—Charge!" As the orders for the smaller units of the brigade rang out, the little command crashed its way through the still-standing dried stalks of a cornfield, keeping up a tremendous racket in the clear, frosty night. So successful was the attack in convincing the Union commander that he was threatened, if not surrounded, by superior forces that Boone hastily moved again during the night, ten miles farther west to Somerville, which he reached at five o'clock on Christmas morning.

Forrest then returned to the critical crossing at Estanaula. Bell's men were there working back and forth across the dark waters by the ruddy light of fires built along the banks and the gleam of a cold moon shining through the bare branches of the giant hardwoods of the Hatchie Bottoms—an eerie sight for the night before Christmas.

Just as Forrest returned to the landing the one frail ferryboat capsized, sending a wagon and a mule team into the river. Wading into the freezing water, he helped to cut the mules loose from their tangled harness. Nearby, on the bank, a newly conscripted soldier declined to help. As a soldier of Forrest's escort remembered the incident, "the recruit was big-mouthed, stompin' up and down, tellin' everybody that he wasn't goin' to get down in that water, no sir, not for nobody he wasn't." Having completed his emergency job with the mules, the general clambered up the muddy bank, quickly stepped up to the grumbler, grabbed him by the neck and the slack of his pants, heaved him high and flung him into the stream. "And after that," the escort soldier remembers, "that fellow made a pretty good hand."

Christmas day was cold and clear. By noon the crossing was completed with all troops, wagons, and supplies on the south side of the river. On the day after Christmas the column was kept busy with maneuvers and skirmishes at New Castle between Bolivar and Somerville. Then moving west he rejoined his wagon train at Whitehall. On December 27, in a torrential rain, the column turned left at Oakland and crossed the Wolf River over a partially burned bridge. By the twenty-ninth, Forrest and his command were safely back in North Mississippi.

No other Confederate commander could have carried out this raid in such an extraordinary manner. He was well on his way toward earning his nickname of the "Wizard of the Saddle!"

THE MAN WHO BURNED JACKSON

Tennessee was the last state to leave the Union on June 8, 1861. Although West Tennessee voted almost five to one to secede, strong pockets of Unionist sentiment remained especially along the Tennessee River. Many of these Unionists became Yankee soldiers. Some of these did so out of a sense of patriotism to save the Union. Others joined up to settle grudges and feuds with their neighbors. The most notorious of these "West Tennessee Yankees" was Fielding Jackson Hurst.

A native of Claiborne County in East Tennessee, Hurst moved west to McNairy County in 1833 and settled at the county seat of Purdy. His position of county surveyor made him familiar with land available for purchase and enabled Hurst, along with his five brothers, to put together such a large block of land that it became known as the "Hurst Nation."

Though Hurst was a slaveowner, he bitterly opposed Tennessee joining the Confederacy and made speeches against secession. For this he was disowned by his friends and neighbors and soon became a target of persecution. In the winter of 1861, he was arrested by Confederate authorities and sent to the state penitentiary in Nashville. In January 1862, he was released only to return home to a scene of destruction. His home had been ransacked. His horses and cattle were gone along with his food supplies, which included several thousand pounds of bacon. Angry and seeking revenge, Hurst organized a company of scouts and enlisted in the Federal army at Trenton under the command of General Grenville Dodge. And, what a sight he was—General Ord laughingly described him as wearing "a tall silk hat, a long coat with brass buttons, baggy jeans pantaloons, and an old sword." Despite his funny appearance, Hurst was given the rank of colonel in the newly organized First West Tennessee Cavalry, and soon proved his worth with his knowledge of the West Tennessee countryside.

By October 1862, Federal commanders were having trouble with Hurst, accusing him of disobedience to orders and threatening to court-martial him. Colonial William R. Morrison, who was stationed at Bethel Station with the First West Tennessee, related his belief that the regiment was "made up of deserters from the Rebels and other bad men." It was "impossible to control them" as some went about the countryside waging private wars with their secessionist neighbors. Most of the regiment's horses had been stolen from citizens, but had since been returned to their owners. However "in most cases," Morrison believed, "people don't complain as they are restrained by fear. These men ought to be removed from here."

News of the First West Tennessee's raiding activities in southwest Tennessee soon reached Major General Grant. The Union commander's irritation with their conduct was reflected in a telegraph to Colonel John A. Logan, the new post commander at Bethel, on October 25: "Complaints are constantly coming to me of depredations committed by Hurst's men on Citizens through the country. They go about the country taking horses wherever they find them. They must desist from this practice or I will disband the whole

Fielding Hurst.

concern. When horses are claimed by citizens, and there is no satisfactory reason why they should be taken, have them returned." Orders were issued for Hurst's arrest, though nothing came of it.

On April 16, 1863, Hurst led a portion of his command to his hometown of Purdy where he ordered the town's citizens to remove the furniture from their homes before he set them on fire. He then gained revenge on his old neighbors by burning the town. One contemporary account described him as playing "the role of Nero" as his troops burned the town buildings, "singing and praying while the church was burning." Even the court record books from the courthouse were destroyed. Federal authorities questioned the authority of such actions, but again no disciplinary action was taken.

On July 12, 1863, Colonel Hurst and two hundred of his men marched with the Third Michigan and Second Iowa Cavalry in an expedition led by Colonel Edward Hatch to Jackson. There they engaged in a running fight with Confederate forces under the command of Colonels Jesse A. Forrest, N. N. Cox, and John F. Newsom. The fight lasted throughout the day as the Confederates retreated up Main Street to a high brick wall near the present location of Jackson Central Merry High School. Here a Jackson woman, Pet McCorry, joined in the fight carrying bullets in her apron. The Confederates retreated east toward the Tennessee River. Hurst followed for eight miles toward Lexington, reporting the capture of twenty prisoners. The citizens of Jackson had been witnesses to the fight with three Confederates killed in the downtown area. They probably breathed a sigh of relief when the fighting stopped, but the worst was yet to come.

Stragglers from the Union expedition soon began breaking into homes and businesses, stealing and burning piles of clothing in the street. The situation got worse when thirty barrels of whiskey were found and passed out to the troops. As the looting grew worse, one store in particular suffered extensive damage—a women's clothing store owned by Mrs. A. A. Newman, a British citizen. She complained to Federal authorities in Memphis that soldiers from Hurst's First West Tennessee Cavalry (later redesignated as the Sixth Tennessee) broke into her business, stole her merchandise, and even took her bonnets to decorate the heads of their horses. Federal authorities investigated the incident and awarded $5,139.25 to Mrs. Newman, which was to be deducted from the regiment's payroll until the payment was satisfied. (Jackson would pay dearly for this a year later.)

On January 11, 1864, Hurst was given a roving assignment to "grub up West Tennessee." As General Sherman put it, "If Confederate sympathizers cannot be made to love us, they can be made to fear us and dread the passage of troops through their country." Hurst certainly made that happen.

On the afternoon of February 6, 1864, Hurst suddenly appeared in Jackson with one hundred of his troops. The reason for his return was obvious. Still angry at his rebuke and fine for the destruction in Jackson, he was determined to get his money back. Gathering up Jackson's most prominent citizens, he threatened to burn the town unless they raised $5,139.25 in United States currency. Twenty citizens promised to raise the money but asked for five days to raise it. Hurst agreed to this condition and went with his command to camp on the property of Bob Chester two miles outside of town. Five days later the money was paid.

Two weeks later on February 25 Hurst returned. Even though the bribe had been paid, his soldiers began setting fires to the buildings on the southeast corner of Lafayette and Market Streets. Before the blazes were finally extinguished, fourteen buildings were destroyed. Many of these buildings could have been saved had Hurst's men not cut the ropes to the town well, which resulted in no water being available to control the damage. It would be long after the end of the war before downtown Jackson was restored.

Hurst continued to terrorize West Tennessee, burning three homes in Brownsville. Strangely enough these homes belonged to Union sympathizers. His acts of destruction seemed without reason. Perhaps the most horrible incident attributed to Hurst occurred in July 1863. A group of Confederate soldiers under the command of Colonel Wharton captured Hurst's nephew William Hurst. Tying him to a tree he was shot between the eyes. Shortly thereafter Hurst captured Wharton and six of his men at Purdy. They were marched south to Pocahontas. For each mile passed, one of them was executed and his body buried along the road as a mile marker. One version of the story states that the prisoners were decapitated and the heads placed on poles as mile markers!

Although Federal authorities seemed to be unaware of Hurst's behavior, Confederate officers were very much aware of his actions. News of the Jackson raid even reached Jefferson Davis in Richmond. On March 10, Nathan Bedford Forrest initiated an investigation into the extortion and burning of Jackson and also of the brutal murders of seven of his soldiers. The results of the investigation were sent by Forrest to the Federal commanders of the Sixteenth Army Corps as follows: "It appears that within the past two months, seven cases of deliberate murder have been committed in this department, most of them and all believed to have been perpetrated by the command of Colonel Hurst. I therefore demand the surrender of Col. Fielding Hurst and the officers and men of his command guilty of these murders, to be dealt with by the Confederate authorities as their offenses require." Not surprisingly, Mayor General Hurlbut chose not to respond.

Forrest's report included accounts of the murders committed by Hurst. The most horrible of these was the torture and execution of Lieutenant Willis Dodds. Captured at his father's home in Henderson County, an eyewitness reported he had been "most horribly mutilated, the face having been skinned, the nose cut off, and the body otherwise barbarously lacerated and most wantonly injured, and that his death was brought about by the most inhumane process of torture."

Guerrilla actions like this were a long way from dreams of the glory of war. However Hurst was burning and killing, a gentler sort of war seemed to go on in other areas. In 1864 Forrest's cavalry nearly caught General Washburn in his nightclothes as he escaped from his room at the Gayoso Hotel in Memphis. Washburn's uniform was taken as a war trophy, but Forrest returned it under a flag of truce. Washburn responded by having a Memphis tailor make a new uniform for his Confederate adversary.

In March 1864, Hurst suffered an embarrassing defeat at Bolivar and his star began to fade. Placed under a general court-martial for failing to follow orders, which allowed five wagons with fifty thousand rounds of ammunition to be captured, he again escaped charges.

To add to his troubles, in July, Brigadier General Edward Hatch launched an investigation into the extortion of Hurst and the Sixth Tennessee against the citizens of Jackson, Tennessee. He reported to Major General Washburn that Hurst claimed the money taken was to compensate his men for the amount taken from their regimental payroll, but Hurst did not share it with his men or turn it over to his superior officers. Instead, he had it deposited with Peter Miller and Company of Memphis, according to Hatch, "for his own private benefit." Hatch demanded that Hurst be placed under arrest and the $5,139.25 be seized. "Undoubtedly there are many unauthorized robberies of this kind, of which Col. Hurst is guilty," Hatch believed.

It is not known what, if any, punishment Colonel Hurst received as a result of the investigation. Five days before the Battle of Nashville, Colonel Fielding Hurst tendered his resignation as commander of the Sixth Tennessee Cavalry. At fifty-three, he was in bad health and was suffering from scurvy, an ailment he contracted while held at the state penitentiary in the winter of 1861–62. His resignation became effective January 8, 1865.

After the war, Hurst's life seemed to return to that of a normal citizen. He was elected to the Tennessee General Assembly representing McNairy and Hardin counties, but resigned after a short time to accept an appointment as circuit judge of the Twelfth Judicial District from Governor William G. Brownlow. President Ulysses S. Grant later made him the U.S. Revenue Collector for Middle Tennessee. In 1876 Hurst and his wife, Melocky, left their home in Purdy and settled in northwestern McNairy County where he died on April 3, 1882. Today Hurst's reign of terror is but a memory. Downtown Jackson is restored and no trace of the fire remains. The historical marker for the Hurst Nation in Bethel Springs on Highway 45 South is our only reminder of Jackson's greatest villian!

17

JACKSON'S MOST FAMOUS DIARIST

obert Henry Cartmell, a Jackson native, kept a diary every day of his life from the time he was twenty-one until his death sixty-five years later! These journals, known as the *Cartmell Diaries*, give a fascinating view of Jackson from 1849 to 1914. His diaries are our best primary source of historical records.

Cartmell was born on July 27, 1828, on the spot where Smith Funeral Home on Main Street once stood. He was educated at old West Tennessee College (now Union) and Lebanon Law School. He was admitted to the Jackson bar, but because of poor health never practiced. Turning to agriculture, he managed the family farm east of Jackson. (Cartmell Street marks this location.)

Following the Battle of Shiloh, Cartmell enlisted as a private in the Fifty-fifth Tennessee Infantry Regiment. He remained in the army for a short period of time before being discharged because of poor health. Despite his efforts to rejoin his regiment, his frail condition kept him out of the army. Returning home, Cartmell found Jackson occupied by Federal soldiers. His diary accounts of Yankee occupation show the hardships of war for families behind the lines. His

Robert Cartmell.

accounts of Jackson in the last two years of the war show how grim life could be. His description of the burning of downtown Jackson by West Tennessee Yankee Colonel Fielding Hurst still gives readers a chill.

Some entries in Cartmell's diary are almost psychic. For example, on April 5, 1862, Cartmell recorded that a large battle was about to take place near Corinth. This journal entry was the day before the Battle of Shiloh. It is curious to note that Cartmell knew about the impending battle while the Federal Commander U. S. Grant did not! In 1859 Cartmell made reference to Jackson's most famous bank robbery when he made the cryptic remark, "Wouldn't they be surprised if they knew who did it!" That secret apparently died with him.

Cartmell was very private about his diaries, never allowing anyone else to read them. He would refer to them for the benefit of others but never let anyone touch them. His desire seemed to be that the diaries remain, after his death, as a historical record of Jackson. Cartmell's diaries are preserved in Nashville in the Tennessee Archives. A copy is preserved at the library here.

The following excerpts are from his diary of 1862 and show what a devastating effect the war had on his life.

FEBRUARY 16, 1862—Confederate General Beauregard in Jackson: "General Beauregard came up on a special train this evening from Corinth is in Jackson tonight. He is a small man, grey hair, dark complexion, would weigh about 130 or 135—large mouth, black eyes, a real Frenchman out and out, restless looking man, quick. He goes to Columbus. The future to us is full of intense interest. God alone knows what that future will bring forth."

MARCH 12, 1862—First Confederate soldiers camp in Jackson: "The Confederate Cavalry or some of them are camped beyond me on the hill right side of the road just this side of the creek."

APRIL 5, 1862—Impending Battle of Shiloh: "Nothing has happened as yet about Corinth, but a battle is not far and a big one it will be not less than 200 or 250 thousand Confederates and 150,000 Federals—we have no fears of the results and hope it will go far to closing this war [in later years the diarist added in the margin here "Too many by a long jump."]

AUGUST 8, 1862—Refuses to take oath of allegiance upon being discharged and returning home: "I had no idea of swallowing an oath of allegiance to the United States, I cannot give an idea of the sad condition of our town and county. The people are suffering in many ways."

AUGUST 23, 1862—Comments on Jackson: "Town—an unpleasant place to the eye and nose."

AUGUST 24, 1862—Comments on Northern troops: "We have to submit as well as we can to our fate. These fellows curse and swear that we brought them down here and ought to suffer for it. They pretend to look upon us as traitors and everything we have as of right belonging to them."

AUGUST 27, 1862—Behavior of Northern soldiers: "In my case if it was not for the restraint held over them by the officers they (the privates) I believe would hang me."

AUGUST 31, 1862—End of August: "I wish this war could close and that war would be no more, here or elsewhere— Farewell August 1862 with a sad heart farewell."

SEPTEMBER 1, 1862—Fire: "Just after dark it was discovered that the house was on fire, on top of the roof, saved some of the furniture, but lost the most of our things."

NOVEMBER 10, 1862—Property destruction: "There was not a rail or garden and the last thing the soldiers did before leaving was to burn up a man's crop of hay worth thousands of dollars. Oh! when will man learn war no more."

NOVEMBER 22, 1862—Illinois soldiers: "The 106th and 95th Illinois Infantry have been encamped between this and town and I think are the worst set of men I ever saw."

DECEMBER 23, 1862—Christmas restrictions: "I have not been to town since last week, no passing is allowed the citizens in town are kept close, no business houses are permitted to be open."

DECEMBER 25, 1862—Christmas Day: "This seems but little like Christmas, no passing in or out of town is allowed. The supplies from the north are cut off soldiers mad and sometimes we think we have more to endure than we can bear. The children in their innocence, playful, noisy renders us happy but God is just and will not chastise us beyond what we are able to endure, we are tired of war, civil war we want to see no more and pray this may soon end, we know not what is going on."

DECEMBER 31, 1862—New Year's Eve: "This is the last day and near the last hour of the year 1862. A year full of events of thrilling interest. History will never record the minute details of this year, and these matters of seeming minor importance are the very things that causes war and should cause it to be dreaded. Could we but picture the reality as it is! It may be well that the veil conceals and will continue to veil many things."

Robert Cartmell, through his diaries, was perhaps our first historian. No other sources contain the information he presented, especially during the Civil War. He had a unique perspective of our history—he was part of it!

18

MEMORIAL DAY 1997

I recently made a speech in Stanton, Tennessee. It was to be a speech honoring soldiers of West Tennessee on Memorial Day. Through Tennessee's two-hundred-year history, our young people have been called to take up arms to defend their country. During the Revolutionary War, the Vietnam War, and the Persian Gulf War, many of these soldiers paid the supreme price, dying in combat.

Foremost in my mind was the Civil War, because of the extraordinary number of West Tennesseeans who were killed. As an example, more soldiers died in the two days of Shiloh than had been killed in all of America's wars prior to that time. Today, with all of our modern weapons, it is unlikely that America will witness a war where large numbers of soldiers fight at close range ever again. From that standpoint, the dead of past wars achieve an even greater historical perspective. To remember their sacrifices is but to honor their memory. What follows is that speech.

Twenty years ago on June 5, 1977, I came to this old cemetery for the first time. I can remember it as if it were yesterday. It was a beautiful hot June day when I was here before and my speech was entitled, "Why We Come Back to Stanton Cemetery." There was a Tennessee Highway Patrolman here that day, standing away from me, at the edge of the crowd. He was watching traffic, and as I began to speak, I decided to see if I could catch his attention. At first I talked louder and soon he began to face me. Then as I lowered my voice, he walked into the crowd and sat down to listen. I knew I was doing all right.

When I came here in 1976, it had been 112 years since Robert E. Lee had surrendered at Appomattox Court House, ending the Civil War. At the beginning of the Civil War Centennial in 1961, I was a senior, a cadet at the Virginia Military Institute. I had breathed the history of the Shenandoah Valley and of Stonewall Jackson and Robert E. Lee for four years. In my junior year, I had lived in Stonewall's own room where he was a professor at the Institute.

In April of 1961, the entire VMI Corps gathered in Richmond to mark the beginning of the four-year centennial. Everywhere, there were thousands of soldiers dressed in their reenactment uniforms. When the parade began, to mark the beginning of the Centennial for all of America, we were the first regiments behind a Civil War band. We could scarcely march, restricted on both sides by thousands of spectators. As we reached the capitol rotunda, where the governor awaited us, the band began to play "Dixie." I will never forget the emotion of that moment as the crowd surged around us. Then I realized how closely the South holds the memories of those four years. I had marched in President Kennedy's inauguration the year before, where I saw John and Jacqueline Kennedy and Robert Frost on the presidential platform. But the memory of that April day in 1961 remains the clearest and haunts me still.

And so today, twenty years later I come again to a special place—to the Old Cemetery at Stanton. But, in some ways, coming back is an enigma. I expected our

The Old Cemetery at Stanton.

fascination with the Civil War to die away after the Centennial. Now, the war has been over for 132 years. And, to my astonishment, our fascination with it is greater than ever.

Last month, on the anniversary of the Battle of Shiloh, authorities had to restrict the number of reenactors. If they had not done so, they would have exceeded the number of soldiers there in 1862. Just this year, two new books on Shiloh have been written, plus a new book on Forrest and one on Sherman. When I heard there was a "new" book on Sherman, I remarked, "how could there be a new book on Sherman—the only thing we don't know is what sort of matches he used in Atlanta." So today, I grant you the fact, that as a Southern people, we do not forget. We will never forget, and how could we forget? For the courage of our Civil War ancestors is the courage we must find again, today, through remembering.

Names like Richard Rowland Kirkland and W. H. Martin, obscure names to most, are names we must never forget for they are the spirit of America. Kirkland was a young confederate in Company G, Second South Carolina Volunteers who found himself behind a stonewall overlooking Fredericksburg, Viriginia. That snowy day, the Federal Army charged up the hill against the stonewall. Thousands of Yankee dead and wounded piled up in front of him. On the day after the Battle of Fredericksburg, he dispensed water and words of encouragement to thousands of wounded and dying Yankees. Known as "The Angel of Mayre's Heights," he was killed in action a year later.

W. H. Martin was a colonel in the First Arkansas in Pat Cleburne's Division. At the Battle of Marietta, in the Atlanta Campaign, gunfire set the woods afire and began to burn alive hundreds of Yankee wounded in front of the First Arkansas trenches. Jumping to the top of the trench with a white handkerchief tied to his ramrod Martin screamed, "We won't fire a gun until you get them away, but be quick about it." The wounded were saved and after the battle, a Yankee major gave him a pair of fine pistols for his efforts. Could we ever forget names like Kirkland or Martin?

Could we ever forget the faces of young Confederates from the Sixth and Ninth Tennessee Infantry? Boys who came from places like Denmark, Jackson, Brownsville, and Dancyville? Boys who were not afraid of war, but afraid the war would be over before they could take part in it. Boys, dressed like men in units with colorful names like the Somerville Avengers, the Dancyville Grays, and the Denmark Danes.

Boys who put sprigs of spring flowers in their hatbands on April 6, 1862, just before dawn at Shiloh and, following two days of that hell, thrown blindly against Federal artillery and the cold steel of bayonets, six hundred of them would never fight again. Every officer of those units, except one colonel, was killed at Franklin. And when the war was over, only one hundred of the Sixth Tennessee and forty of the Ninth Tennessee were left intact. No, for such a sacrifice as that, we never forget. We never quit coming back to these sacred places. And the ladies of the United Daughters of Confederacy never forgot. For more than a hundred years they have kept our history alive. Taking care of the old soldiers, building monuments at Shiloh, Jefferson Davis's birthplace in Kentucky, and Robert E. Lee's home in Arlington, Virginia. Without their work at McGavock Cemetery at Franklin, the dead of that battle would be buried under the asphalt of a McDonalds restaurant. Places like this cemetery will always be remembered.

But today, as we come back, as we come back again, I propose that we remember in a different way. The dead of that war, and of all wars, died for us. And to remember them is for us to stand tall and to be the best that we can be. The tragedy of the Civil War is the forging of America. Through their sacrifices, we became the strongest country in the history of the world. To fail them now would be to forget their memories.

The Civil War is long gone. The sound of artillery, the rattle of musketry, is but a gentle whisper in our minds. But on this Memorial Day, we hear it still.

As the soldiers of the Civil War declined in numbers and grew into old men, they began to reflect about how they would be remembered. Dallas Musgrove, a private in the Fourth Kentucky Cavalry wrote in his memoirs, "Old Soldiers, Confederate and Federal—they are all old—are accustomed to salute the one, the other and exclaim, 'We are passing away. When all shall have answered the last role call, no sculptured marble shall perpetuate the memory of their soldierly witness, but their names shall be enshrined in the memory of their countrymen.'"

In 1889, twenty-five years after the Battle of Gettysburg, a Yankee general named Joshua Lawrence Chamberlain returned to pay homage to the dead. As a colonel from Maine, he had saved the Union army on the second day of the battle producing the inevitability of Pickett's charge two days later. Speaking then and remembering he uttered these words:

> But these monuments are not to commemorate the dead alone, death was but the divine acceptance of life freely offered by every one. Service was the central fact.

> In great deeds something abides. On great fields something stays. Forms change and pass; bodies disappear; but spirits linger, to consecrate ground for the vision-place of souls. And reverent men and women from afar, and generations that know us not and that we know not of, heart-drawn to see where and by whom great things were suffered and done for them, shall come to this deathless field, to ponder and dream; and lo, the shadow of a mighty presence shall wrap them in its bosom, and the power of the vision pass into their souls.

19

JACKSON'S GOLD RUSH

Some things get better with time, some don't. In simpler times, we didn't have many bank robberies. Decades would go by without a bank robbery. A popular myth once said that Jackson was immune to armed robberies because of the myriad of train tracks that surrounded the downtown area. Surely no fleeing robber could risk being stopped by a train. As the railroads declined and branch banks sprang up everywhere, things changed. Bank robberies then became a more frequent occurrence.

Jackson's most famous bank robbery occurred on February 3, 1859. At that time, the Jackson branch of the Union Bank was located where the new Southern Hotel now stands. George C. Miller served as the bank clerk. Miller lived in an apartment in the rear of the bank. Apparently someone that Miller knew well persuaded him to open the vault that night so that he could cash a check. When Miller's back was turned, the assailant struck him in the back of the head repeatedly with a heavy hammer used to hand cancel checks. Miller's body was found the next day. A partially burned check the robber had written was found in the bank's fireplace. The key to the door to Miller's

Ten dollar gold piece.

lodging was placed under the pillow of Miller's bed and the criminal escaped.

Robert Cartmell, Jackson's famed diarist, wrote of a certain person who committed the crime. Being a good lawyer, he did not name the person even in his private diary. Jackson's newspaper, the *West Tennessee Whig* said "the truth will out." So far, one hundred and forty years later, the truth has not come out. The story does not end here however. On September 12, 1985, workers for the city of

Jackson uncovered a cache of gold coins while preparing ground for a new parking lot on West Main Street. The site is located between Autotech and the Midtown branch of First American Bank (now AmSouth). All of the coins were dated prior to 1860, and amounted to approximately twenty thousand dollars—the same amount stolen from the bank.

Within forty-eight hours coin dealers from as far away as the west coast were in Jackson purchasing coins. The street value of these coins exceeded a million dollars. The city of Jackson sued to recover the coins since they were found on city property. By then the coins were too far gone and the suit was lost.

Many speculate on why the robber never returned to dig up the money. Surely he was desperate to commit such a crime. But these were desperate times. Two years later the Civil War began. Perhaps he was killed in the war. It appears that the lot on West Main Street was owned by a director of the bank. Perhaps he committed the crime. Maybe someday we will know the rest of the story.

CASEY'S LAST RIDE

A recent article in *Forbes Magazine* listed Jackson as one of the twenty-five fastest growing cities in the United States in terms of industrial job creation. Though we were twenty-fifth on the list, we were in good company along with cities like New York and Dallas. Much of our industrial growth has come from our rich background of highly skilled laborers from the days when "the railroad was king." As the railroads began to decline, a large supply of industrial labor became available.

Two individuals stand out as the most prominent or powerful men in Jackson's railroad history. One of these was Judge Milton Brown, a lawyer, congressman, and railroad president. His vision helped to bring the Mobile and Ohio Railroad to Jackson; he was president from 1856 to 1871.

The other individual was I. B. Tigrett who began his career in 1912 as president of the forty-nine mile Birmingham and Northwestern Railroad. By 1945 he had become the president of the Gulf, Mobile and Ohio, and Alton Railroads with 2,908 miles of track linking the Great Lakes to the Gulf. Despite the prominence of Milton

Casey Jones.

Brown and I. B. Tigrett, only one name comes to mind when famous railroaders are discussed. His name, of course, is Casey Jones.

John Luther Jones grew up in Cayce, Kentucky. He was nicknamed Casey because of the Kentucky town where he lived as a small boy. During the days when Casey was an engineer, there were no automobiles or airplanes. The engineers who handled the powerful locomotives were folk heros. By April 1900, Casey was feeling the pinch of needing extra money to keep up with expenses for his family. To save money, he planned to move his family from Jackson to Memphis.

On the night of April 30, 1900, Casey brought his train No. 2 into the Memphis station on time. Finding a fellow engineer ill, Casey volunteered to double up, but only if he could drive his engine the Cannonball. This engine was outfitted with Casey's personal whistle. Sounding like a whippoorwill, residents along the route could recognize Casey's whistle when his train went by. He was so punctual that some said they could set their watches by it.

Casey took his fireman Sim Webb with him. They left Memphis sixty-five minutes behind schedule. With Webb pouring the coal to the engine and with Casey at the throttle, they were back on time as they neared Vaughn, Mississippi. Fourteen miles from Vaughn they came up on a freight train on their tracks. Seeing the cars ahead, along with warning rockets, Casey yelled, "Jump, Sim." Webb escaped the fiery crash that followed. When Casey's body was found, one hand was on the whistle and the other on the air brakes. Sim Webb remembered that as he jumped Casey held down on the whistle in a long piercing scream, hoping to warn the freight conductor in the train ahead. No one else was killed.

On May 10, the Illinois Central Railroad reported that Casey was solely responsible for the collision and awarded Sim Webb five dollars for bodily injuries sustained during the wreck. Three other railroad employees were injured and received settlements, one for twenty-five dollars and two for one dollar each.

Several weeks after the wreck, William Saunders, an oil-wiper in Canton, Mississippi, started the song that would make Casey famous. It remained an uncopyrighted folk ballad until 1909, before it became a vaudeville hit. Soon versions of the song were being sung throughout the country.

In 1950, on the fiftieth anniversary of Casey's last run, Jackson celebrated with the issuance of a commemorative postal stamp. In the Casey Jones Village, one can visit Casey's home along with many of his personal effects. In addition there is a replica of his Cannonball Express Engine and a whistle similar to Casey's. Clark Shaw and Associates have done a wonderful job keeping Casey's legend alive.

Though controversy swirled around the wreck, Casey became one of America's true folk heroes. Jackson's heritage is richer for it. Casey's famous whistle is rumored to be in a private collection in St. Louis. Perhaps some day we can bring it home to Jackson where it belongs.

Do you remember the "Ballad of Casey Jones?" This is the first verse:

> Come, all you rounders, for I want you to hear
> The story told of a brave engineer;
> Casey Jones was a rounder's name
> On a heavy six eight wheeler he rode to fame.

JACKSON'S UNSUNG HERO

Jackson has its share of heroes and famous people. One of our most famous individuals is relatively unknown. His name was Samuel C. Lancaster. Born in Magnolia, Mississippi, in 1864, Lancaster's family moved to Jackson when he was a small boy. His father lost most of his money in one of the financial panics following the Civil War. As a result, it was necessary for Lancaster to seek employment after finalizing just one year of college at Southwestern Baptist University (now known as Union University).

As the eldest of five children, he took an engineering job with the Illinois Central Railroad to help support the family. In addition to his work he continued his engineering studies. While doing railroad construction work he contracted malaria in the Yazoo, Mississippi Delta. Coupled with the long hours he was working, the malaria turned into infantile paralysis (polio). His recovery from this disease is a remarkable story of courage and determination. For eighteen months Lancaster lay in bed, able only to move his head. A doctor, convinced that the paralysis was complete, tried sticking needles under his fingernails. Howling with pain, he never forgot how much that hurt.

Sam Lancaster.

Still, his fingers, toes, and limbs were crippled and bent out of shape. As his tendons began to harden, he was haunted that he would end up as an exhibit in circus sideshows.

He began his recovery by concentrating on moving the middle finger of one hand. Eventually he was able to place a pencil in his month. In this manner he learned how to write, this time without hands. Unable to stand, he designed a frame with ball bearings for wheels. Each day his family strapped him into it and gradually he was able to move around the house. The exercise, though painful, gradually enabled him to walk with crutches. At this point some city officials came to him for help on an engineering project. Though his fingers were still crippled, he was able to complete the required drawings, holding the pencil in his mouth.

Although still crippled, he was hired again as a resident engineer with the Illinois Central Railroad, serving in this capacity from 1884–1885. During this period his health returned to normal. Heading west in 1886 he served as resident engineer with the Gulf Colorado and Santa Fe Railroad and then with the Texas Pacific Railroad.

Returning to Jackson he was employed as the city engineer from 1888–1906. In addition, he was the superintendent of the Water and Light Plant from 1893–1906 and served as the chief engineer for the Madison County Good Roads Commission from 1903–1905. His work in Madison County led to so much acclaim that he was appointed as a consulting engineer with the Office of Public Roads in Washington. His work in Jackson was finished, but his greatest achievement was yet to come.

Moving to Seattle, Washington, he was first employed as a consulting engineer for highway construction. From 1908 until 1910 he was professor of highway engineering at the University of Washington. During this time, Lancaster met a wealthy individual named Samuel Hill who would have a lasting influence on his life. In 1908 Hill invited Lancaster to accompany him to Europe where they were delegates to the First International Road Congress in Paris. On this trip Lancaster studied roads in the Rhine Valley built centuries ago by Charlemagne. Five years later, through Hill's influence, Lancaster was invited to fix the location and direct the construction of a highway through the gorge of the Columbia River. This road was named the Columbia River Scenic Highway. It would become one of the most famous highway projects ever built in America. It would later be called Lancaster's Road in his honor. In a sense, he was building more than a highway. He was building a legend. It was to be his ultimate achievement, his memorial. To build a road over the mountain heights seemed impossible. Only Lancaster's vision and determination made it possible. In one section, engineers were lowered on ropes for two hundred feet, hanging like spiders over the Columbia River. The Scenic Highway was opened on July 6, 1915, between Portland and the Hood River. Two months later the extension to the Pacific coast was opened. Today modern highways have replaced most of Lancaster's Road. He is still remembered as the one who made it possible.

Today Lancaster is remembered as the engineer for the Columbia Highway, America's greatest highway through the Cascade Mountains to the sea. In Jackson he was honored when Lancaster Park was named for him. This park occupied fifty-four acres of land on North Royal Street adjacent to the newly built electro-chalybeate well. (A Tennessee Historical marker is on the site today.) Like his famous road, Lancaster Park is but a memory. Today few people recognize the name of Samuel Lancaster, even though he remains one of our most famous citizens.

HISTORIC WOMEN
OF JACKSON

Jackson has been fortunate to have many women who played a large part in our history. What follows is a brief description of some of them.

Jane Donelson Hays was the sister of Rachel Jackson, the wife of Andrew Jackson. Married to an officer who fought in the Revolutionary War, she moved here as one of our earliest settlers. She had three daughters and two sons who were nieces and nephews of "Old Hickory," Andrew Jackson. One daughter married Dr. William Butler, considered to be Jackson's founder. Another daughter married Colonel Robert I. Chester, our first postmaster and U. S. marshall. Because he had family here, Andrew Jackson gave special attention to this city named for him. His presence is still felt here, generations later. Descendants of Jane Hays, like the Edentons and Stegalls, still live here.

Sue White was active in the fight for women's voting rights. She was a member of the National Woman's Party. On February 10, 1919, White, along with sixty-five other women, burned an effigy of President Woodrow Wilson in front of the White House. She was arrested and jailed for this, but soon released. White was the only Tennessee

Emma Inman Williams.

woman to be arrested during the suffrage movement.

Margaret Brown came to Jackson in 1830 as the wife of one of our earliest physicians. She was called the patroness of flowers because of her yard and gardens. Sarah Paralee Porter was the wife of an Officer in the Mexican War. She was the first female Tennessee librarian, serving from 1871 to 1879. The McCorry sisters—Ellen, Pet, and Musidora were prominent during the Civil War and afterwards in the reconstruction period. The United Daughters of the Confederacy named their Jackson chapter for Musidora McCorry when it was organized in 1894 with Belle K. Allison as its first president. A second chapter was organized in 1925 with Miss Laura Bishop as president. The Daughters of the American Revolution began here in 1901 with Mrs. Harriet Holland as the first regent. Miss Hettie Harris was the first president of the Mutual Improvement Club in 1893. A year later, Mrs. J. H. Hunter became the first president of the Ingleside Book Club. These organizations continue today.

Miss Alice Drake served as Jackson's librarian for almost a half century. She served as our first librarian when the Carnegie Library was opened shortly after the turn of the century. Beginning with five hundred books, the library collection grew to more than fourteen thousand books by the time she retired. During the winter of 1918, the library furnace blew up. The library was without heat for six weeks in the most bitter cold weather in Jackson's history. Through her determination to serve the public, the library stayed open with a small kerosene stove as the only heat.

When I think of the library, another name comes to mind. Emma Inman Williams was reference librarian in the Tennessee Room from 1973 to 1986. Prior to this she had a long career as a history teacher at Jackson High School. In 1946 she published *Historic Madison* and later co-authored *A Pictorial History of Jackson-Madison County.* Our best historian, she was named Woman of the Year in 1979 by the Altrusa Club.

Another teacher was Camille Bright Bell. She taught English in the city schools for fifty years, beginning in 1885 at the old College Street school. Serving under six superintendents, she was an inspiration for the children she taught. Near the close of her career she said, "My work has been a labor of love. You know I have ever adored children above all else. It has been the supreme joy of my life to be with them, to instruct, to sympathize with them in the schoolroom."

Maybelle Louise Smith was know to the rhythm and blues world as "Big Maybelle." In 1935 she was discovered by Jackson promoter Dave Clark. She was fifteen years old at the time, and Clark first heard her sing at the Rock Temple Church of God In Christ on South Highland. A recording artist for King and Decca labels, she packed night clubs for more than thirty years. In 1952 she recorded the original version of "Whole Lotta Shaking Going On," later made famous by Jerry Lee Lewis. These are but a few of our famous ladies who have been a part of our history.

THE GIRL WHO DANCED
IN THE MOONLIGHT

One of my favorite stories about Jackson is of a book written seventy-five years ago. The name of the book is *The Windy Hill*. The main part of the book describes an incident which occurred on the author's farm on Cotton Grove Road when a girl danced in the moonlight.

Harriet Clay Long was born one hundred years ago in 1901. Her friends called her Hattie Clay or Clay. She attended city schools in Jackson and then Union University. She was the star dancer at Jackson social events. Leaving Jackson behind in 1924, she became a star dancer in New York in Earl Carrol's Vanities, a popular dance revue.

Clay was the daughter of James H. Long. Long owned the Amour Hotel, formerly known as the Central Hotel near where the Barrel Wine and Spirits Company on West Chester is now located. As a young man, Long used to drive a wagon around town. People were used to yelling "wo boy" at him and thus he became known as "Wo Boy Long."

Before she moved to New York, every man in Jackson seemed to be in love with Clay Long. Her diary tells of days when she would have dates with four different boys and even six on one occasion. She was the center of attention in

Jackson's social life. Stunningly beautiful, she was the queen of Jackson. In September 1924, Clay made front-page news in New York when an infatuated admirer killed himself because she would not marry him. Her biggest adventure, however, occurred not in New York, but in Jackson.

In June 1924, Clay went for a late night rendezvous with three male friends. The destination was a hill east of Jackson. Today you would know it as the big hill just north of the East Union Community. (Though many call it an Indian mound, it is a natural volcanic structure standing high above the fields around it.) On a whim, and as a farewell gesture to one of the boys who was moving away, Clay took all of her clothes off and danced nude in the moonlight. It was a moment they never forgot. (I know two of them and they still talk about it seventy years later.)

It was a special night and they vowed to keep it a secret. But the story got out. Two years later, to their shock, a book appeared entitled *The Windy Hill*. Thinly disguised, it was a novel of life in Jackson with the four of them as the primary characters. The title referred to Clay's dance. It was the focal point of the book.

The book caught Jackson by surprise and created a sensation. Perhaps today such an act would not create the stir it did in 1924, but back then no one was dancing in the moonlight with her clothes off. People still remember hiding the book from their parents. Others remember their parents burning the book. (Perhaps that is why it took me so long to find a copy.) The author of the book was Jennings Perry. He was the same age as Clay and, like her, attended Jackson city schools and Union University. He was a writer for the *Jackson Sun* and a reporter for the *Commercial Appeal*. Later he became the associate editor for the *Nashville Tennessean*. When the book came out he left Jackson and spent a year traveling in Africa. It would be the only book he wrote. He died in 1987 and is buried in Jackson.

Hattie Clay Long.

Long after the book came out Clay married Lawrence Garland, a railroad attorney, and lived in Anna Marie, Florida. When her husband died she moved back to Jackson. She died in 1982 and is buried in Riverside Cemetery.

The Windy Hill describes a carefree time in Jackson, six years after the boys came home from World War I. The railroads were king and life was full of fun and prosperity. It is a wonderful book of Jackson in the 1920s. But most of all, it is the story of a girl who danced in the moonlight.

THE DAY THEY
CLOSED THE BANK

M any people in West Tennessee remember when bank
examiners swooped into town in late October 1990,
and closed the First National Bank of Jackson. Ernest
Vickers, president of the bank, served a jail sentence for his
role in the bank's failure. Future historians will look back
at this event as one that occupied newspaper headlines for
months. Still, if you were not an investor, no loss came to
the bank's depositors when First Tennessee assumed the
assets of the failed bank. Today, except for their headquarters building, now occupied by another bank, there is
little evidence of their existence.

Nearly three quarters of a century ago, in June 1925, a
banking crisis in Jackson occurred with worse conse-
quences. No historians have told this story. Emma Inman
Williams has only a two-sentence reference to it in *Historic
Madison*. Even though her book was first published more
than twenty years after the bank failed, the story was still
too sensitive to talk about. Too many prominent people
were involved!

The Federal Deposit Insurance Corporation (FDIC) was
not chartered until 1933. Thus, people who had money in

their bank account were not insured as they are today. Loss of confidence in a bank could cause a "run on a bank" when a large number of customers become frightened and withdrew their money. If enough people withdrew their money, a bank could fail.

Problems for the Peoples Savings Bank of Jackson began in the second week of May 1925, when state bank examiners discovered a shortage of $342,000. T. B. Carroll, executive vice president and cashier, assumed full responsibility for the shortage. In addition, overdrafts of $21,750 were uncovered for J. W. Ross, a federal judge in Memphis. Ross was a partner of Carroll's in business ventures, reputed to be land speculation in Florida.

The Peoples Savings Bank was Jackson's most prominent bank. In 1924 they moved into their new building—Jackson's most modern office building and only skyscraper. You would know that building as the former home of First American Bank, located downtown at the corner of Highland and Main Street which was destroyed several years ago to build the new city hall.

Newspaper accounts in the *Commercial Appeal* give a somber description of the last days of the bank. H. B. Oliver, state bank examiner in charge, gave the following description.

> The run that started early Monday morning and which officers of the bank believed they had stemmed, persisted yesterday and today. As the flood of checks and passbooks continued to come in the cash on hand dwindled to less than $4,500 at one time yesterday. A heavy draft then would precipitate the closing of the bank.

> As the outflow continued today the situation took on a somber hue. Mr. Oliver held frequent conferences throughout the day with the officials and as a last resort hung out the closing sign.

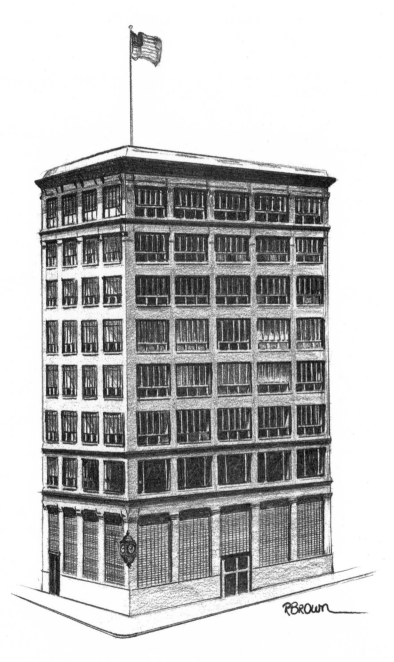

First National Bank Building.

As a result of the bank's failure T. B. Carroll and his son John M. Carroll (also a bank officer) were indicted on charges of bank fraud. The trial was held in the first week of January 1926. A special edition of the *Jackson Sun* was printed on January 4, 1926, with large headlines stating "T. B. Carroll Submits: Gets Three Years—Indicted Ex-Banker Pleads Guilty To Charges of Fraudulent Breach of Trust." The state was represented by Attorney General Tom Murray, while Carroll was represented by Hu C. Anderson. (Anderson was a judge in the Nuremberg trials of Nazi war criminals following World War II.)

Other prominent figures were involved. Clarence Pigford, owner of the *Jackson Sun*, had served as the president of the bank for six months prior to its failure. It is unlikely that he could have had any knowledge of the bank's failure.

Judge Ross remained silent on the affair despite demands for his resignation as a federal judge. On July 9, 1925, his body was found under his overturned car in a canal five miles from Jackson on the Miflin Road. We will never know whether he committed suicide or was the victim of an accident.

Through the actions of the directors many depositors recovered their money. Some did not and lost their life savings. When T. B. Carroll was released from prison, he sold his home at 1287 Hollywood Drive, known as Green Gables, and moved his family to Memphis.

BIG CROWDS IN JACKSON

M onday, August 19, 1996, was a big day in the history of Jackson, Tennessee. Other U.S. presidents had been here before, but this was the first visit ever of a president while he was in office. It does not matter whether you are a Republican or a Democrat or whether you like or dislike the Clinton-Gore team. It was a day that future historians will recall when the president plus the vice president and their families were here.

The crowd was estimated to be more than four thousand. If you were in the traffic jam along U.S. 70 West or in the mob at McKellar Airport, you probably felt like the crowd was much larger. The August heat along with the claustrophobic conditions helped to give that impression.

From a historic perspective, however, other occasions in Jackson have produced much larger crowds. In 1870, Jefferson Davis, the president of the Confederate States of America, made his first speech here after being released from a Federal prison. The crowd was so large that the meeting was moved from St. Lukes Church to a site near General Samuel Hays's home at the corner of Preston and North Royal Street.

In 1884 and again in 1893, a Methodist revivalist
named Sam Jones produced tremendous crowds in downtown Jackson at the corner of Liberty and Chester Streets.
More than ten thousand people listened as he preached
against whiskey proclaiming, "I believe that if the devil
himself were president of the United States, and if there
was no whiskey, he would resign and go back to hell within
three weeks!"

The most popular historical person to visit Jackson was
General Andrew Jackson, for whom this city was named.
Jackson's sister-in-law Jane Donelson Hays lived here.
Thus he was the uncle of her five children, all of whom
played a prominent part in Jackson's early history. "Old
Hickory," as he was called, first visited here in 1825, prior
to going to Washington as a United States senator. After a
welcome given by the Jackson Lodge No. 45 of local
Masons, he made a speech in front of the courthouse.
Fifteen years later, as an old man, Jackson returned again
in October 1840. By this time, he had served two terms as
president and four years as advisor to his successor Martin
Van Buren. Jackson's wife, Rachel, was dead and he was
suffering from broken ribs. More than ten thousand people
gathered at the grove on North Royal Street just north of
the fairgrounds.

It was an eloquent speech, reminiscent of General
Douglas McArthur's farewell address at West Point. In his
speech Jackson said, "It is probably the last time that I
shall have it in my power to exchange salutations with you.
. . . The infirmation of age admonishes me, that I can not
much longer be a partner with you in the vicissitudes of this
life." It was to be Jackson's last visit here.

A number of prominent politicians have campaigned
in Jackson. On October 21, 1860, Stephen A. Douglas
spoke here. He had been nominated for the presidency by
the Northern Democrats and the issue of the day was
slavery, which he supported. He was destined to loose to
the Republican candidate, Abraham Lincoln. Robert

Cartmell, Jackson's famed diarist, was opposed to Douglas and reported that only five hundred people turned out to hear him. Cartmell said he could not support any man who favored the expansion of slavery. Henry W. McCory reported that Douglas was hissed at when he arrived at the train station, and that it would have suited him if Douglas only spoke for six minutes. And yet another in the crowd that day, a Mr. Anderson from Brownsville, reported that a crowd of more than seven thousand gathered in front of the courthouse to hear "the greatest living statesman of the day." Such diverse views are the nature of Southern politics!

William Jennings Bryan was the Democratic candidate for president in 1896, 1900, and 1908. Though he lost all three times, he was considered to be one of the most powerful speakers of his time. He spoke in Jackson in the early 1880s when he was first being mentioned as a presidential prospect. Bryan drew a huge crowd at a site across the street from the First Methodist Church.

The 1960s would see three politicians of national prominence come to Jackson. Senator Lyndon B. Johnson of Texas was campaigning for the vice presidency in 1960 on the Democratic ticket with Sen. John F. Kennedy of Massachusetts when he spoke at Court Square in front of the New Southern Hotel. Just a little more than three years later he was to become president when Kennedy was struck down by an assassin's bullet in Dallas. In that same year, former President Harry Truman was hosted at a luncheon at the New Southern by Governor Buford Ellington after Truman addressed a big crowd at Trenton to solicit votes for the Democratic ticket of Kennedy and Johnson. His efforts were only partly successful—Kennedy carried Gibson County but lost in Madison and statewide to the Republican nominee, Richard Nixon.

Richard Nixon, at that time a former vice president and a private citizen, climbed onto a makeshift speaker's stand in the lobby of the New Southern Hotel in 1966 when rain

Lyndon B. Johnson at New Southern Hotel.

cancelled a scheduled Court Square Republican rally. Nixon had come to Jackson to speak on behalf of GOP candidates Howard Baker for the U.S. Senate, Julius Hurst for Congress, and G. H. Berryhill for the state legislature. Baker and Berryhill were elected.

Two years later, Vice President Hubert Humphrey made a "non-political" address in Jackson as the keynote speaker for the Salute to Higher Education observance. His visit came just weeks after President Johnson announced that he would seek re-election and a couple of days before Humphrey formally tossed his hat in the ring for the nomination he received at the stormy Democratic National Convention in Chicago.

In 1972 Alabama Governor George Wallace, a Democratic candidate for president, addressed a big crowd at the airport on the eve of Tennessee's first presidential primary. The people of Madison County responded to Wallace's candidacy by giving him nearly 74 percent of the vote as he swept the state by slightly smaller margins. Nineteen days after Wallace's visit to Jackson he was struck down by an assassin's bullet while campaigning at a shopping center in Laurel, Maryland.

In 1998, Jackson had a political double header when two Democratic nominees for president spoke here on the same day. Reverend Jesse Jackson was first, followed about an hour later by Gary Hart. A large crowd of several thousand people gathered in front of the courthouse to hear the two candidates. Jackson was already the crowd's favorite with his fiery manner of speaking. He closed his speech by asking everyone to hold up their hands. When they did so, he responded, "These hands that once picked cotton in Tennessee will help today to elect a president of the United States!"

Though many famous politicians have come to Jackson, Bill Clinton remains as the only president to visit here while he was still in office. Perhaps future editions of *Historic Madison*, the book about Jackson's early history, will include August 19, 1996.

COPS AND ROBBERS

Jackson is full of history. Large portions of it can be found in *Historic Madison*, the book written by our best-known historian Emma Inman Williams. There is much of our history, however, that is not covered in that book. This history is harder to uncover. Current historians have to go back to early cemeteries, census tracts, and old newspapers. Jonathan K. T. Smith is one such Madison County historian who has done much to preserve the history of Riverside Cemetery. Another is Chris Malone, a member of the John B. Ingram Camp of Sons of Confederate Veterans. Active in the Historic Riverside Cemetery Walk, Chris became interested in one of Jackson's early police chiefs, Tom Gaston. This story comes from his research.

Gaston was born in Columbus, Mississippi, in 1862. His father died when Tom was a small boy, and his mother then moved the family to Jackson. When he was twenty, he joined Jackson's police force. This early police force had four members, responsible only for the enforcement of city ordinances. The county sheriff and the city marshall were responsible for the keeping of law and

Tom Gaston.

order. Gaston remembered the only thing he did of importance during this period was arresting a man who set a local Santa Claus on fire!

Gaston was a rough sort of fellow who could handle himself well in a street fight. He got a number of chances to prove this toughness in arresting drunks in the local saloons. His reputation began to grow when he arrested a man named John Teague. When Teague refused to go to jail, they fought with fists, guns, and knives. Gaston got bruised up, but Teague was transported to jail unconscious.

In 1888, Gaston was promoted to the position of lieutenant of police. The next summer he got his first real test when he confronted a gang who intended to free a friend in the local jail. Gaston knew that the jail was the sheriff's business but said, "the street belonged to me." When he faced the gang, he was struck by a shotgun blast that ripped through his left eye. Returning fire, he killed one of the assailants and wounded the others. Found lying in a pool of his own blood, a doctor removed sixteen slugs from his body. A slug in his left eye was left there because of its proximity to the brain. It would torment him for the rest of his life.

Gaston soon established a reputation for his marksmanship with a pistol. A favorite trick was to place a piece of tape over the hole in a washer. Tying the washer to a string, he would have someone swing it back and forth like a pendulum. A lighted candle was placed behind it. Shooting through the tape on the swinging washer, the bullet would extinguish the candle flame! His reputation for doing this kept other toughs from testing him.

One individual had no respect for Tom Gaston. His name was W. C. Strickland, the owner of one of Jackson's cheaper saloons. Strickland was in constant trouble selling liquor to minors and for illegal gambling. Choosing to pay the fines, he continued to defy the law while running his saloon. Things came to a head when he elected to defy local ordinances and kept his bar open on Sundays. Knowing that Gaston would come after him, he had a brass bullet proof vest made for him at the local Mobile and Ohio Railroad shop. To increase his chances, Strickland had his brother hiding in a building across the street with a pistol. When they squared off, on Sunday, December 21, 1892, Strickland drew his pistol first. Before he could fire, Gaston shot him in the forehead. As Tom recalled, "I sent him to Hell, where he belonged." The brother fired and missed and was later arrested. Strickland's family tried to have Gaston tried for murder. After a jury trial of seventeen days, he was acquitted. Gaston was involved in a number of other gunfights. He was shot so many times that area newspapers simply reported, "Gaston shot again."

Besides serving as police chief, he was later appointed as fire chief. With the help of Mayor Hugh Anderson, he was responsible for the installation of electric fire alarms throughout the city. He bragged that, because of the alarms, they never let a fire get out of control. He also served as a member of the local draft broad during World War I. In addition, he was both president and secretary of the West Tennessee Fair Association for many years.

On February 23, 1918, Tom Gaston was found dead in his room at the Southern Hotel. A blood clot from the old wound in his left eye had caused him to suffer a fatal stroke. He was fifty-six. He is buried at Riverside Cemetery.

Two of America's most notorious criminals have come through Jackson. One was alive, and one was dead. George "Machine Gun" Kelly came here in September 1922. For a short period of time, he was the most wanted criminal in America. Kelly, known in those days as George K. Barnes, was arrested by Chief of Police Tip Taylor. Barnes's companion was a man named P. G. Hammond, who was also arrested when they stopped for a meal at the Fox Restaurant. Chief Taylor noticed the car with out of state license plates which seemed to be loaded down. When he checked the car, he found that it was filled with bonded whiskey. Since it was unlawful to transport whiskey across state lines, the two were arrested and taken before Judge R. N. Barham. Kelly, alias Barnes, was fined one hundred dollars and sentenced to sixty days in jail.

On February 2, 1947, the Sun Chaser, the Illinois Central's train from Florida to Chicago, stopped in Jackson at 9:30 A.M. Excited citizens were allowed on the train to view an expensive bronze casket containing the body of Al Capone. Capone, once America's most famous gangland leader, had died at his estate in Miami and his body was headed for burial in Chicago.

THE CITY OF JACKSON
FIRE DEPARTMENT

The city of Jackson has fifteen fire trucks in six separate stations. Their annual budget is in excess of six million dollars; the Madison County Fire Department has sixteen stations located throughout the county with 172 fire fighters and sixty-one pieces of equipment. Fighting fires is a big business. One can only imagine what life was like before we had professional fire fighters.

Jackson was organized in 1822. One of the first city ordinances listed a five dollar fine for anyone who tied matches or other combustible materials to a dog or cat's tail and let them run through the city. If a fire broke out, the only hope was for neighbors to put it out with buckets of well water.

During the Civil War, Colonel Fielding Hurst, a Yankee from McNairy County, threatened to burn the town if a five thousand dollar ransom was not paid. Even though the ransom was paid, his soldiers cut the ropes to all of the wells and burned much of the town. It would be more than twenty years after the war before all of the buildings were replaced.

In the early 1870s the city bought a hand-drawn and hand-operated pump to be manned by volunteers. This was the beginning of the volunteer fire department. Eight years later it was sold for twenty dollars!

On March 8, 1882, the mayor and the Board of Aldermen had a special meeting in which they resolved that new fire fighting equipment needed to be purchased, that more water cisterns needed to built and placed around the city, that two volunteer companies should be organized to take charge of the new equipment, and a new fire alarm bell should be hung in the courthouse as soon as possible. One week later the Jackson Volunteer Fire Department was created by ordinance. Ham King was elected as the first chief. (King was one of Jackson's most prominent citizens, having twice served as mayor. He owned King's Palace, a saloon and billiard hall on Market Street, Jackson's most prominent saloon. Anyone

Early Jackson fire engine.

campaigning for political office in West Tennessee was sure to stop there.)

On March 20, the city voted to purchase twenty-eight hundred dollars worth of new fire equipment which consisted of:

1. A Number 5 Champion Chemical Fire Engine;
2. One hook and ladder truck;
3. One hand hose reel;
4. One Button hand water engine and five hundred feet of 2½-inch hose.

All of this equipment was designed to be hand drawn and hand operated by the volunteer firemen. Horse-drawn engines would come later. The equipment arrived in Jackson on May 20 with crowds of people on hand to see it.

Excitement over the new fire department and its equipment ran high, but sobering circumstances soon followed. Less than two months later, an arsonist set several fires in downtown Jackson, and on July 15 he attempted to burn down the finest block of buildings in the city. The Memphis *Commercial Appeal* reported the next day that "Jackson was being infested by a arsonist. . . . Jackson now has a fire engine, but has no cisterns adequate to its needs, and now water works are wanted to save the place from the incendiaries that infest it." A vigilance committee was formed and the fires stopped, though the arsonist was apparently never caught.

On September 16, tragedy struck when volunteer fire fighter Peter Cook was killed. The accident occurred on Market Street when Cook fell off the engine while it was en route to a fire. He was crushed beneath the wheels and died the next day. He was Jackson's first fire fighter killed in the line of duty. He was buried in Riverside Cemetery.

Enthusiasm for the fire department diminished after Cook's death, and Chief King had difficulty finding enough volunteers to pull the engines. With the excitement of a fire, he could usually get enough people to pull the wagon to the fire, but getting it back to the station was a problem. In his annual report to the city council, dated January 28, 1884, King resigned saying, "So I can't see any use of a chief without men, as the only thing I can do is look after buildings and stove pipes, flues and dangerous combustibles, and if it was a paying office, I would advise you to abolish it. Thanking you for the honor you bestowed on me and hoping you will find a better man for the place."

In 1885 the city of Jackson completed its water works at a cost of one hundred thousand dollars. It consisted of two pumping engines with a capacity of one million gallons each, and nine and one half miles of mains. Fire hydrants were placed on most of the city street corners thus eliminating the necessity of hand pumping. Thomas M. Gates was elected as volunteer chief in 1885, serving until February 1888 when he resigned. Frank F. Reavis then was appointed to succeed Gates.

Reavis was somewhat of an activist and petitioned the city council for new equipment and improved conditions. He advised against the practice of burning trash in the streets and leaving construction material on the sidewalks. Farmers who left their horse-drawn wagons unattended for hours proved to be an additional obstacle. The city council did nothing about these suggestions. In his annual report in 1889 he chastised the council saying, "You have no idea what a laughing stock your companies are. They received in return for their services, ruined clothing and the ridicule of many of your best citizens. All matter of fun is made of them . . . No city or town ever had a poorer equipped nor a harder working fire department than this city. They are all good men and deserve the praise and thanks of the entire community." After making further recommendations, Reavis resigned in frustration.

In early 1893, the city finally established a paid fire department. Tom Gaston, the police chief was appointed as the first paid fire chief. As police chief, Gaston was paid sixty dollars a month. By taking on the additional duties as fire chief, he received another fifteen dollars. The next year his salary was reduced from fifteen dollars to ten dollars a month! Two additional firemen were paid forty dollars a month. Thus Jackson's first paid fire department operated on salaries of less than one hundred dollars per month!

As a new century approached, the department moved to horse-drawn wagons. The early fire horses were kept at King's livery stable on Main Street between Highland and Shannon. As the horses grew older they were retired and relegated to pulling the city garbage wagons. Still they remembered their days with the fire department. Upon hearing the fire alarms, they would race to the fire, spilling city garbage all over the streets. During this time the city established nineteen electric pull alarm stations throughout the city. Keys were kept at nearby houses.

Between 1890 and 1900 the population of Jackson doubled in size from ten thousand to twenty thousand inhabitants, forcing the city to improve its fire fighting capabilities. Several large fires also prompted them to seek improvements. Large fires occurred at the Jackson Woolen Mills in 1897, the Pythian Opera House in 1901, the main building of Lane College in 1904, and the Nashville, Chattanooga & St. Louis Railroad in 1910. In 1912 the city bought an American LaFrance Pumping Engine for nine thousand dollars. This was the first motorized fire engine in the state of Tennessee.

In 1915 the city council's form of government was changed to a commission. One of their first acts was to elect Ben L. Warlick as fire chief at ninety dollars per month. Amazingly he served in this position for almost sixty years, retiring in 1974. Three members of the Williams family were members of the fire department from 1900 to 1979. Between them they had 130 years of service.

Today Jackson and Madison county have one of the best fire departments in the Mid South. When you see a fire engine heading toward a fire, think back to earlier days when horse-drawn engines raced to a fire or to even earlier days when sweating firemen raced through town pulling engines. We have come a long way.

28

THE BOONE TREE

ackson and Madison County is rich in its history. The first settlers came here in 1819. Since that time many of America's famous characters have passed across our stage, from Davy Crockett to Casey Jones. Of our early frontiersmen, none could surpass Crockett. Jackson would play a large part in his life. When he was defeated here in 1835 by Adam Huntsman in a race for the U.S. Congress, Crockett left Tennessee in an angry mood. A year later he was dead at the Alamo. Of the early hunters on the frontier, only Daniel Boone was more famous than Crockett. When you think about Boone, you normally associate him with the settlement of Kentucky in the 1700s. Recent studies show that Boone traveled as far west as Idaho. Perhaps he hunted and camped in Madison County along the way.

In June 1968 two Lambuth College (now University) teachers were looking for an Indian mound on the Warmath Farm on the Old Medina Road near Oakfield. The two were Dr. George Edwards, a science professor, and Dr. Marvin E. Eagle, a history professor and dean of the college. Dr. Edwards's son Tom was present also. They found a small knoll with a large beech tree on the top of it. Years later an

archeologist took core samples from the knoll and determined that it was a natural formation and not an Indian
mound. But the beech tree on the top was quite a surprise.
Carved on it were the words "D. Boon" and the date 1776.
The initials E. B. and M. C. are also carved on the tree. Boone
had a brother named Edward and a friend named Micajah
Calloway who was the brother of Boone's son-in-law,
Flanders Calloway. Edward Boone and Micajah Calloway
were frequent companions of Boone on his hunting trips. The
initials E. B. and M. C. are enclosed in a square below the
D. Boon inscription. Two half moons are carved in front of
M. C. Half moons are pioneer or Indian symbols to show how
many weeks had passed since the hunters left home. A half
moon means two weeks, so two such signs would mean they
had been gone for four weeks. Also carved in the tree is either
a deer or a bearskin. Another figure is a B with a large tail
which could indicate the hunters found beaver on the nearby
Okeena River, later to be named the Forked Deer. At a later
time Dr. James Warmbrod, a University of Tennessee forester,
took core samples from the tree and found the healthy part
of the tree was over three hundred years old. Only half of the
original tree remains, so it was surmised that the tree could
be over five hundred years old! At the time of the discovery,
Edwards and Eagle surmised that the carvings were no more
than the work of a prankster. Still the carvings aroused the
curiosity of Dr. Edwards. For more than thirty years he
explored the surrounding area while researching Daniel
Boone's life and travels.

Tennessee history is relatively silent about Daniel
Boone. Only one historical marker mentions him and this is
located in far away Washington County near Johnson City.
It marks the site where Boone hid under a waterfall to
escape an Indian raiding party. Nearby is a beech tree with
the inscription "D. Boon cilled a bear in year 1760." No
other Tennessee record is found of him.

Daniel Boone was one of the most famous pioneers and
trailblazers in American history. James Fenimore Cooper

Henderson then sent Boone and thirty woodsmen to improve and connect the Indian trails and buffalo paths reaching into the heart of Kentucky. This route became known as the Wilderness Road. That same year he chose a site near the Kentucky River to build a fort called Boonesborough near present-day Lexington. After building a cabin there he returned home to bring his family to Kentucky. His wife and daughter were the first white women to enter Kentucky. Frontier life was difficult for the settlers, for they had to endure constant fighting with Indians.

In 1778 Boone was captured by Shawnee Indians but was soon adopted by Chief Blackfish who named him Big Turtle. Months later he escaped and returned to Boonesborough, covering 160 miles on foot in four days! His return helped warn the settlers of an impending Shawnee attack. After days of fighting the Indians withdrew. In 1782 Boone lost another son, Israel, in Indian fighting.

By the mid-1780s Boone was one of the richest men in Kentucky, owning more than one hundred thousand acres of land. Better at fighting Indians than lawyers, Boone lost all of the land in legal battles and was in debt. In 1779, at the request of the Spanish governor who controlled the territory, Boone led a group of settlers into Missouri. When asked why he was leaving Kentucky, he gave his famous reply: "Too many people! Too crowded! Too crowded! I want more elbow room!" Settling within sixty miles from St. Louis, he was awarded a land grant of 850 acres, and soon received even more land when he brought in one hundred new families. Soon, the territory became part of the United States under the Louisiana Purchase in 1803. Boone lost all of his land again. In 1814 Congress restored his 850 acres, but creditors soon stripped it from him.

Rebecca Boone died in 1813, and though his life was nearing an end, Daniel continued to wander. When he was well past his eightieth birthday, he journeyed more than eight hundred miles through the wilderness all the way to the Rockies. Striking overland from there he spent the winter camping on the Yellowstone River. Returning at last to his home in Missouri, he died in the summer of 1820.

The site of the Boone tree is about six miles north of where Campbell intersects with Highland, where The Hut Restaurant used to be located. The Old Medina Road is an old Indian trail that went past the site. One branch of the road went to Paris in Henry County. Another branch extended to Reelfoot Lake. The Middle Fork of the Forked Deer River lies close by.

Dr. Edwards, who continued his search for Daniel Boone artifacts in Tennessee, found another beech tree with the initials E. B. on it. Presumably this would be Edward Boone, Daniel's brother, whose initials are also on the first tree. Carved beneath the initials is an arm and hammer symbol. Also included in the group is an upside-down bottle and an indistinct carving which resembles a head. The empty bottle would represent the end of the journey.

If Boone came to West Tennessee it would have occurred in the fall of 1776. On September 7, 1776, Colonel Arthur Campbell sent a supply of shot and powder overland from the Holston Valley for Boone to distribute to settlers fighting the Indians. Having finished this task, it is likely that Boone would have continued exploring and hunting into West Tennessee along the south and middle forks of the Forked Deer River.

John Bakeless of Pasadena, California, wrote the definitive biography *Daniel Boone: Master of the Wilderness*. Dr. Edwards sent Bakeless pictures of the carvings. In 1969 Bakeless wrote Dr. Edwards as follows: "The tree-ring count, which does not exist for any of the other carvings, is especially valuable. I have very little doubt of the authenticity of these carvings."

In Louisville, Kentucky, there is a museum maintained by the Filson Society. (Named for the first historian of Kentucky.) The museum maintains another Boone carving taken from a beech tree. It was carved by Boone in 1803 and is nearly identical to the Madison County carving.

One notable exception is that Boone had now added the letter "e" to his name.

In addition to the two Boone trees, Dr. Edwards found yet another beech tree with carvings. This tree has the initials J. R. and H. R. carved on it, with a figure of a man with a surveying instrument carved beneath it. Though this tree has no connection to the Boone carvings, it has a great deal of historical significance. In 1783 North Carolina was one of the last states to cede her western lands to the federal government. In 1785 North Carolina sent surveyors into the "Western District" to locate and survey land grants they had given. James Robertson, Henry Rutherford, and Edward Harris were selected. (Robertson is often called the "father of Middle Tennessee." On Christmas Day, 1779, he was one of a group of settlers who founded Fort Nashborough, now Nashville.)

They left Nashville in canoes and descended to the mouth of a small river that empties into the Mississippi. The Indian name of the river was Okeena, but they changed the name to Forked Deer because of a deer they killed with unusual shaped horns. Rutherford surveyed lands adjacent to the Forked Deer, while Robertson surveyed along the Obion and Loosa Hatchie. During this trip more than 360,000 acres were surveyed. Robertson and Rutherford made the first maps of West Tennessee. There can be little doubt that the Rutherford and Robertson site is authentic. But what about the Boone trees? There is no definitive way to prove that Daniel Boone was here in 1776. And yet, all of the evidence makes it seem likely. Perhaps further historical research will one day give us a more definitive answer.

29

A FOOTBALL GAME
OF LONG AGO

September approaches and with fall comes the football season. As John Ward, longtime announcer for the Tennessee Volunteers used to say, "It's football time in Tennessee!" Recently the author purchased an old football program by way of the Internet. The cost was ten dollars. Fifty-eight years have passed since that game was played, but the program looks like it was printed last week. The date was November 14, 1942, and the game was played at McGugin Field in Nashville. The two teams were Vanderbilt and Union University.

Today we think of Union as a school with a rich basketball tradition. Few people remember or know of their sixty years of football history. Beginning in 1893, they played their first game against Ole Miss, loosing 56–0. It was the first game for Ole Miss also!

The Japanese attack on Pearl Harbor had occurred on December 7, 1941, eleven months before the game was played. The cover of the program reflected the wartime sentiments of the day. The program showed the "Star Spangled Banner" with the Washington Monument and the Statue of Liberty; planes were shown flying beneath

Union vs. Vanderbilt.

the American flag. Inside the program, a list of former Vanderbilt players indicated those in service. Two of those former players were listed as killed or missing in action.

Because of the war, both teams had limited numbers of players. Union had thirty-three while Vanderbilt had forty. The players were smaller then. Vanderbilt had only two players who weighed more than two hundred pounds. One of those was Charlie Hoover, a freshman from Jackson. Playing center, he was six-foot-four-inches tall and weighed 213 pounds. He was the tallest and heaviest man on the team. Today he is remembered as one of

Jackson's most outstanding athletes and is a member of our Sports Hall of Fame. Walter Kilzer, longtime coach at Trenton and the University School of Jackson, was a sophomore and one of Vanderbilt's star players. Oddly enough, Union did not have anyone from Jackson on their team. Harry Johnsey, a longtime Jacksonian, was listed as an assistant coach, though he had enlisted in the navy prior to the beginning of the season. The mid-November game was the eighth and next to last game of the season. Union, with nicknames of the "Bull Pups" or the "Cardinal and Cream," had quite a record before traveling to Nashville. They lost the first game of the season to Mississippi State 35–2, and then won the next six games by a combined score of 174–0!

Leading the offense for Jackson was James "Casey" Jones a senior from Florence, Alabama. Weighing only 170 pounds, he was a little All-American tailback who could run, pass, or kick. "Red" Sanders, the Vanderbilt coach, said, "Casey Jones was one of the greatest backs ever to perform at McGugin Field." In Union's first six games, Jones had personally accounted for sixty-eight points.

Union used an offense called the "Notre Dame box shift." This offense had been introduced to Union in 1935 by a new assistant coach who was a recent graduate of the University of Alabama. His name was Paul "Bear" Bryant. A star athlete at Alabama, Bryant turned down numerous offers to play professional football. Union was his first job as a coach in what would be one of the greatest coaching careers in football history. His salary was $170 per month! While in Jackson, Bryant and his wife lived in a garage apartment at the corner of West King and Highland. (His daughter was born there.)

Union was not to win that game, even though Casey had a great day with runs of thirty-eight and fifty-two yards. The final score was Vandy 27 and Union 0. In the last game of the season, Union defeated Tennessee Polytechnic

Institute at Cookeville to win the S.I.A.A. Conference title. It had been a great year for Union and for Casey Jones, despite losses to Mississippi State and Vandy. I can only guess what the attendance was that day—not much by today's standards. But for those who were there, and for those who played, it was a wonderful interlude when the horrors of World War II seemed far away. Union continued its football program for ten more years, playing its last game in 1952.

FOOTBALL AND TURKEYS
World War II Christmases in Jackson

hristmas should be a time of peace. Christmas should be a time for families to gather together at home to celebrate the most blessed of seasons. Hopefully Christmas will be a time of peace for most of the world. Unfortunately there have been many years when war overshadowed the Christmas season, and our young men were far away. World War II was such a time. It is appropriate to look back at those wartime Christmases and see how it affected Jackson.

1940

Christmas of 1940 arrived as all of Europe seemed to be going up in flames, and the United States tottered on the brink of war. Perhaps because of the chaos around us, and the uncertainties ahead, Christmas that year seemed to be a little brighter, the parties to last a little longer, and the abundance of food and gifts available seemed to be endless. It revealed the true meaning of Christmas, a Christmas that would set the standard for holiday celebrations for years to come.

In 1940 Tennessee football was at an all time high. Headed into the Rose Bowl at Pasadena, they were undefeated in the last twenty-three games and no opponent had scored against them in fifteen straight games. Nevertheless, they would lose to Southern California 14–7 on January 1, 1940. During the next ten games Tennessee was again undefeated and ranked number one in the nation. Only two teams, Alabama and Virginia, managed to score on them. This time they headed to New Orleans and the Sugar Bowl. Boston College pulled off a huge upset and beat them 19–13 on New Year's Day, 1941. Van Thompson of Jackson was a starting tailback and safety. He scored one of Tennessee's touchdowns.

Excitement ran high on December 22 when the city of Miami train came through Jackson with 254 passengers. It left Chicago at 9:40 A.M. and arrived in Miami twenty-nine hours later. On the night of December 22, a nativity scene was staged at First United Methodist Church. Vincent Watson was director of Music and Mrs. J. T.

McClaren was organist. Another nativity scene was located at Alexander School. The *Jackson Sun* noted that visitor Dr. Loring Clark, rector at St. Luke's Episcopal Church, declared that Jackson, with its gala lighting and decorated streets, was the most attractive city from here to Los Angeles.

All of the grocery stores advertised Christmas specials: eggs twenty-nine cents a dozen; select oysters thirty-three cents per pint; ham sixteen cents per pound; six foot Christmas trees fifty-nine cents. And for those who needed to do last minute shopping, plenty of gifts were still available. At Holland's, suede jackets were $4.95; Pearl and Lowenstein's layaways were fifty cents a week; Tuchfelds's satin gowns cost seventy-nine cents; Grand Leader's scooters were thirty-nine cents; Rosenbloom's blankets started at $1.99; Kisber's had men's shirts at one dollar; Stegall's had men's shoes by Jarman for five dollars; McGee Ross sold a fifty-seven piece buffet service for $3.95. Chesterfield Market, McCall Hughes, and G. H. Robertson advertised large stocks of goods at low prices. College students streamed home for family celebrations—Rhea Dabney and Thomas Hart were among the college students coming home. Both of these young men would be killed before the war was over. A December 24 headline of the *Jackson Sun* read: "Hitler Plots Invasion of England." But at the New Southern Hotel, holiday menu featured oysters or shrimp for the first course with a choice of trout, lamb, turkey, steak, dover sole, chicken or omelet, for the main course. The price was $1.00 per cover!

On Christmas Day, Dr. and Mrs. Jere Crook entertained in the morning with eggnog and beaten biscuits at their home. While in the afternoon, between five and six, Mr. and Mrs. Clarence Pigford served eggnog and fruit cake at their home. (Now the site of the First Presbyterian Church.) On Christmas night at 7:00 P.M. the

Bal Masque had a supper buffet and dance at the Gold Room of the New Southern Hotel. The dance just finished in time for hotel employees to clean up for the Kappa Chi formal to be held in the same place. Also, on Christmas Day a La Juenesse benefit ball was held at the National Guard Armory.

1941

December 7, 1941, brought the flames of war a lot closer and America was in the war for good. By Christmas time, food was still plentiful but prices were climbing. Ham was twenty-seven cents per pound, up from sixteen cents per pound the year before. Eggs climbed from twenty-nine cents a dozen to thirty-nine cents and oysters were up from thirty-three cents to thirty-nine cents a pint. McGee Ross advertised roller skates for ninety-eight cents a pair and a Betsy Wetsy doll for only $1.98. G. H. Robertson advertised men's shirts for two dollars, double the price from the year before. A bank was constructed on Main Street for the sale of liberty stamps and bonds. Judge Walter Baker Harris, as a small boy, helped to raise $24,500 in sales. There were not so many parties that year. Only the Theta Kappa Omega (TKO) dance at the New Southern Hotel was reported by the paper, though ads to "Dine and Dance" at the Chickasaw Club to the music of Charlie Baker were frequent. J. E. Underwood, minister at First Methodist, preached a sermon entitled "Christmas Reminders" to remember the true spirit of Christmas. The Boy Scouts collected paper for national defense while more than one thousand young people benefited from the Rotary Club Christmas tree sale. Though much still appeared normal on the surface, in many ways daily life had changed forever. The *Sun* reported that Lt. Joe Crook was safe in the Pacific, but two brothers from Humboldt, Cecil and Milton Kennington, were killed at Pearl Harbor. It was just the beginning. Christmas Day was clear and mild that year with a low of forty degrees and a high of sixty-three degrees.

1942

Eggs, as an economic indicator, were up again, rising from thirty-nine cents to forty-five cents a dozen. Spam and souse were mentioned in grocery ads for the first time and turkey was at forty-three cents a pound. Chesterfield Grocery, Jackson's gourmet food market, still advertised oysters, shrimp, fresh crab meat, and Spanish mackerel but not the prices. Tuchfelds was a big advertiser with ladies' evening dresses that cost $8.95. Santa Claus couldn't deliver much candy that year because of sugar shortages. Only one party was reported—the annual New Year's Eve party at the country club. Four bank robbers were caught in Jackson after they tunneled into the vault of the Bank of Gadsden and stole $250 in nickels and pennies! No telegrams were allowed that year for Christmas greetings, which was a popular practice in past years. President Franklin Roosevelt said "to fight, work and save," and the *Jackson Sun* headline on Christmas Eve stated, "The Observance of Christmas Will Be a Somber Affair as Our Thoughts Will Be with the Boys." Christmas Day was warm and clear with lows in the fifties and highs in the sixties.

1943

Christmas treats were hard to find in 1943 and expensive. Chesterfield Market advertised only ocean perch and mackerel. Oysters were up to sixty-three cents a pint and turkey was up to fifty-two cents a pound. Kisbers dominated the retail market with seventy-three clerks and a slogan of "You Never Pay More At Kisbers." Citizens were asked to open their homes to soldiers. Somber headlines announced

rationing beginning on January 1 and warned of huge casualties in the next ninety days with the invasion of Europe.
Dwight Eisenhower was made supreme allied commander on
Christmas Eve. Christmas Day in Jackson was cold with
temperatures in the twenties and a light dusting of snow.

1944

The best thing about Christmas of 1944 was the
weather, especially for those who wanted a white
Christmas. There were two snows that week, both light.
Food prices continued to rise. Oysters skyrocketed to
seventy-one cents a pint. Turkeys were fifty-one cents a
pound. Few retailers advertised specific products that year,
mainly because retailers' supplies were limited. The
National Bank of Commerce suggested its customers buy
war bonds with their Christmas money. Christmas Day
started with rain but turned to snow.

1945

Christmas of 1945 was almost like Chrstmas of old.
Historians raised twenty-five hundred dollars to print the
first edition of *Historic Madison*. The First Methodist
Church had a Christmas Eve service at 11:00 P.M. along with
First Presbyterian, First Christian, and Lambuth Memorial.
Soldiers streamed in from every port in a desperate attempt
to get home for Christmas. Scores of couples announced
engagements and dances were beginning again. Christmas
dinner would be special with many families complete for
the first time in many years. The Beare Company advertised
"Happy Times are Here Again." Christmas day was warm
and rainy.

LOOKING BACK
Christmas a Half Century Ago

Although we were at war again in 1950, this time in Korea, Christmas with all of its magic was near at hand. It started on December 1 when the Chamber of Commerce held its annual Christmas parade. Twenty-five thousand people jammed downtown Jackson for the start of the season. As always, Santa Claus appeared in his sleigh to the delight of the children. By December 20, prospects for a white Christmas looked good as temperatures dropped into the teens. December 22 marked the official start of winter. It was the shortest day of the year and temperatures held in the 20s.

Far away in Korea, Christmas was not so bright as American soldiers fought for their lives. The Korean War started on June 25, 1950, when troops from Communist-ruled North Korea invaded South Korea. The war would last for three years. In late November, China sent a huge force against the Allies. Four days later twenty thousand American marines and infantrymen were trapped on the Chongjin Reservoir. By Christmas Eve, 105,000 U.S. and Korean troops had been evacuated by sea from the port of Kungman. Headlines in the *Jackson Sun* reported that,

"Americans Facing Christmas Seriously with Their Minds on GI's Fighting in Korea." Other stories brought the names of Jackson soldiers who were casualties. PFC Thomas A. Dugger was listed as wounded. He was the first volunteer from Jackson to enlist when the marines began their recruiting drive here. Major Walter T. Warren was also listed as wounded. The article in the *Sun* continued, "American's in the midst of plenty face Christmas seriously this year with their minds on fellow countrymen fighting in Korea's barren wastes." Shops were never more abundant. Yule decorations never more lavish. But an outward air of Christmas cheer would not obscure ominous world events and thoughtfulness at what the future might hold. The grim outlook placed added emphasis on home ties as Americans across the country gathered for Christmas reunions.

But Christmas will always be Christmas, no matter what world events bring. City and country schools let out on December 20 and would not reopen until January 2. The college crowd was on its way home. Oliver Benton was home from Vanderbilt while Marion White, Eliza Stone, Edward Hazlehurst, and Donald Stegall were home from the University of Tennessee. There were numerous opportunities to celebrate. Tony Wald and his orchestra were playing at The Pit, a restaurant and dance hall on Highway 45 South. Admission was $2.40 per couple. Peggy McKinnie joined Jimmy Allen for a "White Christmas" concert and Elizabeth Ingram's dance and speech students gave a concert at City Hall on December 21. A Christmas party for children was held at the Malco Theater. Admission was one box top from Hadicol, a popular medicine for "tired blood." The child with the most box tops received a free Schwinn bicycle. Two movies were shown, one with Hopalong Cassidy and another with Woody Woodpecker.

Sports and hunting were in full swing. The Kentucky Wildcats' football team was headed for the Sugar Bowl under Coach Bear Bryant. He smugly reported that his team looked so good, they didn't need to practice any more! Coach Bob Neyland and the Tennessee Volunteers were headed to the Cotton Bowl. Wrestling was also popular then. Farmer Jones, a local favorite and a hog farmer from Arkansas, was to wrestle Finis Hall from Great Britain on the night of December 21. Other favorites were Roy Welch and Red Roberts. They were listed as "the wild men of the square ring." (Farmer Jones won and gave Hall "the licking of his life.")

The hunting season was in full swing. Most popular were quail, rabbit, or duck hunting, since turkey and deer would not be plentiful in West Tennessee for years to come. With cold weather and plenty of water, duck hunting was at its best. Picket Reasonover, an outdoor writer, reported that Gabe Allen, Joe Patton, Bill Lawrence, Burton Gillman, and Mike Tucker were "calling the ducks in over the decoys." Sauger fishing was good on the Tennessee River, if one could stand the cold!

Downtown Jackson was at its peak with Christmas specials in every store. Allen's Appliance offered a new model black and white television for $362.34. John E. Parker had Schwinn tricycles for $5.95. A set of eight Christmas lights cost 69¢. The *Jackson Sun* was full of ads. The Christmas Eve paper had eighty-eight pages. Stores now long gone wished everyone a Merry Christmas. Hollands, Tuchfelds, Kisbers, and Rosenblooms offered clothing. Perel and Lowenstein had watches for $19.88. McGee Ross offered an eight-place dinner set for $29.95. Beare Ice and Coal advertised they were on every corner with ice for holiday celebrations. The S. M. Lawrence Company offered coke and coal to keep you warm. The Fox Restaurant and The Hut offered holiday dining. Grocery specials for Christmas items were as follows: coconuts were two for twenty-nine cents, oysters were seventy-nine cents a pint, and turkey was forty-nine cents a pound. Simpson's Grocery advertised cranberry sauce for ten cents. If you

needed a ride to a store all you had to do was call Hub City Cab at 7-3311.

All three local banks had large ads wishing everyone the best of the season. The National Bank of Commerce (now Union Planters) invited everyone to open a Christmas club account, even though they paid no interest on them and charged fifty cents if you didn't make all the payments. Even Robert Mainord, the chief of police, took out an ad wishing everyone a happy holiday.

On Christmas Eve, the *Jackson Sun* carried a lengthy article speculating on what the year 2000 would bring.

Among the predictions were that the United States would have a female president, a manmade star circling the earth, and World War III with Russia.

By Christmas day the weather moderated with temperatures near 60 degrees. There would be no white Christmas. Christmas was quieter that year with concerns about our boys in Korea. And yet, in many ways, it was the best of Christmases. For in the celebration of the birth of a child in a manger in Bethlehem, hope shined brightly for the last fifty years of the twentieth century.

THE MAN WHO
WAS SANTA CLAUS

George Smith became mayor of Jackson in 1943. He was only thirty-three years old and the youngest mayor in Tennessee. Over the next thirty-two years he served four terms totaling sixteen years as our mayor. He was one of our strongest mayors. But today he is best remembered in a different way. For almost half a century, he was Jackson's Santa Claus.

As an elected official, he did not have to become a soldier in World War II. He elected, however, to serve his country and spent eighteen months in the Medical Corps at Massachusetts General in Boston, Mass., and later in Abilene, Texas. He remained as Jackson's mayor during this time but refused to be paid.

In 1945, when he returned home, he began his career as Santa Claus. Purchasing a Santa Claus suit, his first appearances were at schools, nursing homes, parties, civic clubs, churches, and industry Christmas parties. His wife, Elizabeth, remembers that he felt called to help people. He loved to make people happy. He loved to see them smile.

As Santa Claus, he made that happen. His suit came from New York. It was made of the finest red velvet with

Santa Claus.

white trim. The beard and wig were made from real hair. Each year after Christmas the suit would go back to New York to be cleaned and stored until November 1 of the next year when it would be shipped back to Jackson. His wife would keep his gloves clean for each appearance. He never wore a watch or rings and his glasses were replaced with contacts. In every way he looked like Santa Claus and the children were never disappointed.

When people called him at home to request an appearance, he would respond with "let me check with old Santa" or "let me put him on the phone for you." Wherever he appeared, he always had sleigh bells in his hand and candy canes on his belt. When children told him their house had no chimney, he would produce his magic key and tell them not to worry. No child ever stumped him. He had an answer for everything. He even had his own North Pole stationery to write children. When he left home, he left George Smith behind. His children say that he honestly believed he was Santa Claus!

For many years he appeared at friend's homes, often for succeeding generations. Dr. Ben House once called to say that his daughter Catherine was "on the fence" about whether Santa was real. The sight of him waving at her through the window changed that. Today, as a grown woman, she says, "because of him, we still believe."

It was a strenuous schedule for him. Each year he would begin his visits on December 1 and continue through December 22. On the last day of school, he would appear at ten different places. There was rarely time to take his wife to Christmas parties. On one occasion he got his schedule mixed up and was to be in two places at the same time. His son Jerry borrowed an outfit and appeared at the Pinson Methodist Church in his place. Jerry remembers that there were 250 children there and they had him sitting next to a red-hot pot bellied stove. Never again did anyone substitute for George. Jack and Jerry remember another occasion at the home of Dr. Charles Cox. When Dr.

Cox's four boys were later asked why they kept staring at Jack and Jerry, they responded they thought they were two of the wise men!

Each year his last appearance of the season would be with Cousin Tuny in the children's wing of the hospital. On one occasion, as he was leaving, a family member asked him to visit his mother who was lying in bed, seemingly unable to speak. When he asked her, "Don't you remember when you were a little girl, I used to bring you fruit and candy." She awoke and responded, "Yes, I remember." He was the magic of Christmas.

Santa's last visit was in 1992 when he came to visit his great-grandson George at the University School of Jackson. He died on Christmas Eve, 1993. There will never be another Santa Claus like George Smith. He kept the magic of Christmas alive for thousands of children. As Christmas approaches, you must ask yourself if you still believe in Santa Claus. I hope you do. Because of George Smith, I still believe.

SELECTED BIBLIOGRAPHY

Alexander, Harbert L. R. "The Armstrong Raid Including the Battles of Bolivar, Medon Station and Britton Lane." In *Tennessee Historical Quarterly*. Volume 21, No. 1, Nashville, Tenn.: N. P., March 1962.

Bakeless, John. *Daniel Boone: Master of the Wilderness*. Harrisburg, Penn.: Stackpole Books, 1959.

Cartmell, Robert. *Diaries 1849–1915*. Tennessee State Library Association (microfilm), Tennessee Room, Jackson-Madison County Library.

Henry, Robert Selph. "First with the Most Forrest." In *Forrest*. New York: The Bobbs-Merrill Company, 1944.

Kwas, Mary L. "Antiquarians' Perspective on Pinson Mounds, Tennessee."*Anthropologist Journal of the Tennessee Anthropological Association*, vol. XXI, no. 2, fall 1996.

Lancaster, Samuel C. *The Columbia—America's Great Highway*. Portland, Oreg.: The J. K. Gill Company, 1926.

Lucas, Rev. Silas Emmett, Jr. *Goodspeed's History of Tennessee Illustrated*, 2nd ed. Easley, S. C.: Southern Historical Press, 1979.

Mainfort, Robert C. Jr. Pinson Mounds—A Middle Woodland Ceremonial Center, Tennessee Department of Conservation, Division of Archaeology, Research Series, No. 7, Nashville, Tennessee, State of Tennessee, 1986.

McCann, Kevin D. *Hurst's Wurst: Col. Fielding Hurst and the 6th Tennessee, (U.S.) Cavalry*. N.p.: Cardinal Press, 1997.

McCann, Kevin D. *The Peg Legged Politician: The Life of Adam Huntsman*. Ashland City, N. C.: N.p.: 1996.

Morgan, Miles Captain. *Jackson Fire Department: A History of Service*. Owatonna, Minn.: Jostens, 1993.

Morton, John Watson. *The Artillery of Nathan Bedford Forrest's Cavalry*. Nashville, Tenn.: Publishing House of the M. E. Church, 1909.

Norton, Mark R. "The Pinson Mounds Complex." West Tennessee Historical Papers, vol. LV, December 2001.

Perry, Jennings. *The Windy Hill*. Chicago: The White House Publishers, 1926.

Smith, Jonathan Kennon Thompson. Mt. Pinson Madison County, Tennessee. N.p., 2000.

———. My Riverside Cemetery Tombstone Inscriptions Scrapbook. 7 volumes, N.p., 1992–1995.

West, Carroll Van ed, *The Tennessee Encyclopedia of History and Culture*. Nashville, Tenn.: Rutledge Hill Press, 1998.

Williams, Emma Inman. *Historic Madison*. 3rd ed. Kingsport, Tenn.: Arcata Graphics, 1986.

Williams, Emma Inman, Marion B. Smothers, and Mitch Carter. *Jackson and Madison County: A Pictorial History*. Norfolk, Va.: The Donning Company, 1988.

Wyeth, John Allan. *That Devil Forrest*. New York: Harper Brothers, 1959.

INDEX

King Recording Studios, 148
King's Palace Saloon, 34, 170
Kinney, Thomas J., 101
Kirkland, Richard Rowland, 130–31
Kisber's department store, 189, 191, 195
Kitty Hawk, N. C., 45, 47
Korean War, 193–94, 197
Ku Klux Klan, 34
Kungman, 193
Kwas, Mary, ix

La Juenesse, 190
Lafayette Street, 117
LaGrange, Tenn., 71
Lambuth College, 175. *See also* Lambuth University
Lambuth Memorial, 192
Lambuth University, 31, 175, 210
Lancaster, E. R., 13
Lancaster, Samuel C., 29, 141–44, **142**
Lancaster Park, 144
Lancaster's Road, 144
Lane College, 173
Laurel, Md., 161
Lawler, Michael, 75, 103
Lawrence, Bill, 195
Leatherstocking Tales, 178
Lebanon Law School, 121
Lee, Robert E., 69, 128
Leggett, Mortimer, 72
Lessenberry, Jerry, ix
Lewis, Jerry Lee, 148
Lexington, Ky., 179
Lexington, Tenn., 91–93, 104, 116
Lexington Road, 92
Liberty Street, 158
Lincoln, Abraham, 158
Lockwood, Greene and Company, 10
Loftin family, 3
Logan, John A., 114
Logan, Samuel B., 102
Long, Harriet "Hattie" Clay, 149–52, **151**
Long, James H., 149
Long, John, ix
Loosa Hatchie River, 181
Los Angeles, Ca., 189
Louisiana, 52, 72
Louisiana Purchase, 179
Louisville, Ky., 180
Lowe, W. W., 103

Madison College, 7
Madison County: Tenn., xi, 1–2, 19, 25, 33, 50, 67; Fire Department, 169; Good Roads Commission, 143; *Herald*, 2
Madison Farmer's Co-Op, 20
Madison Grays, 59
Magnolia, Miss., 141
Main Street, 116, 121, 154, 173, 190
Maine, 132
Mainfort, Bob, ix
Mainord, Robert, 196
Malco Theater, 194
Malesus, Tenn., 3

Malone, Chris, 163
Manassas, Battle of, 70
Manifest Destiny, viii, xi
Marietta, Battle of, 130
Market Street, 117, 170–71
Marshall County, Miss., 59
Marshall County Museum, 61
Martin, W. H., 130–31
Mason, Joseph, 9
Masons: Denmark Lodge, 5; Jackson Lodge No. 45, 158; Lodge No. 193, 7; Pinson Lodge, 14
Mason's Wells, 8–9
Massachusetts General, Medical Corps, 199
Mathis, Dave, 97
Matthews, Mark, 9
McArthur, Douglas, 158
McBride, Archie, 21
McCall Hughes, 189
McClaren, J. W., 31
McClaren, Hilda, 188–89
McClellan, George, 69
McClellan, Isabella, 36
McClellan, James Dixon, 36
McClellan Road, 36
McClung, Colonel, 59
McCorry, Ellen, 34, 147
McCorry, Musidora, 34, 147
McCorry, Pet, 34, 116, 147
McCorry, Henry W., 34, 159
McCoy, Reverend John, 13
McCulloch, Robert, 71–72, 78
McGavock Cemetery, 131
McGee Ross, 189–90, 195
McGugin Field, 183
McKellar Airport, 157
McKenzie's Station, 102
McKinnie, Peggy, 194,
McKissack & Burton Grocery, 5–6
McKnight family, 3
McLean, Milton, 43–44
McLemoresville, Tenn., 103
McNairy County, Tenn., 2, 113, 120, 169
Medon, Tenn., 3, 73–76, 78
Medon Academy, 3
Memorial Day, 36, 127, 132
Memphis, Tenn., 5, 20, 65, 67, 107, 109, 119, 139, 154, 156
Memphis & Charleston Railroad, 71, 109
Memphis & Ohio Railroad, 100
Memphis Conference Female Institute, 31
Mercer, Bank of, 4
Mercer, T. B., 3
Mercer, Tenn., 3–4, 6, 20
Mercer Opera House, 4
Meriwether, James, 8
Meriwether and Jett Hotel, 5
Meriwether family, 8
Meriwether's Store, 6
Methodist, 3, 5, 8, 13, 33, 36, 49, 158
Mexican War, 34–35, 59, 61, 63, 67, 147
Mexico, xiii, 65, 67
Meyers, William E., 15

Miami, Fla., 167, 188
Middleburg Road, 72
Miflin Road, 156
Miller, George C., 133
Miller, Mary Louisa Blount, 56
Miller, Pleasant, 56
Mississippi, 52, 69, 210
Mississippi Central Railroad, 6, 70, 73, 90
Mississippi Regiment, 59–60
Mississippi River, 19, 52, 105, 107, 181
Mississippi State University, 183, 185–86
Missouri, 179–80
Mobile & Ohio Railroad, 2, 6, 14, 35, 81, 90, 97, 99–100, 102, 137, 166
Monterrey, Battle of, 59
Morrison, William R., 114
Morton, John W., 109
Moscow, Ky., 102
Mount Pinson, 13–17
Mt. Olivet Cemetery, 30
Murrell, John A. , 21, 42, 49–53, 56, **51**
Murtaugh family, 8
Musgrove, Dallas, 132
Mutual Improvement Club, 147

Nashville, Battle of, 119
Nashville, Chattanooga & St. Louis Railroad, 173
Nashville, Tenn., 49, 52, 90, 114, 181, 183, 185
Nashville Tennessean, 150
National Bank of Commerce, 192, 196
National Congress of Mothers, 35
National Guard, 5, 56
National Guard Armory, 190
National Register of Historic Places, xi, 15
National Woman's Party, 145
Neely's Store, 6
Neill, E. F., 31
New Castle, Tenn., 112
Newman, Mrs. A. A., 117
New Orleans, La., 52, 65, 67, 69, 188
Newsom, John F., 116
New Southern Hotel, 133, 159, 189–90, **160**
New York City, N.Y., 137, 149–50
Neyland, Bob, 195
Ninety-fifth Illinois Infantry, 125
Ninth Tennessee Infantry, 131
Nixon, Richard, 159–60
North Carolina, 178, 181
North Highland Avenue, vii
North Korea, 193
North Royal Street, 157–58
Norton, Mark, ix
Notre Dame, 185
Nuckolls, John, 15

O. G. Gardner Lumber Company, 4
Oakfield, Tenn., 175
Oakland, Tenn., 112
Obion County, Tenn., 43

ABOUT THE AUTHOR

Harbert Alexander attended public schools, graduating from Jackson High School in 1957. He graduated from the Virginia Military Institute in 1961 and has a graduate degree from Rutgers University. He served as an artillery officer in Schweinfurt, West Germany, retiring from the army as a captain. He was associated with Jackson National Bank for twenty-four years, serving as president of the bank and vice chairman of the holding company. He was appointed president and CEO of Union Planters Bank of Jackson in 1988.

In 1998, Mr. Alexander was promoted to the regional president's position for all of the West Tennessee and Arkansas Union Planters Banks. He was appointed to the position of executive vice president and regional executive in charge of all Union Planters Banks in Arkansas and Mississippi effective July 2001.

On January 1, 2002, Mr. Alexander stepped down from his regional duties but remains chairman of the board of the Jackson, Tennessee, bank. He serves as Madison County historian, chairman of the board of Lambuth University, and is a member of the Jackson Utility Division board. He was chosen to be the Jackson's Exchange Club's "man of the year" in 1991. He is married to Nora Noe and has three children and two grandchildren.